Cambridge Elements

Elements in Public and Nonprofit Administration
edited by
Robert Christensen
Brigham Young University
Jaclyn Piatak
University of North Carolina at Charlotte
Rosemary O'Leary
University of Kansas

MANAGING PUBLIC SECTOR CONTRACTS

Market Frictions and Human Resources Solutions

Matthew Potoski
University of California, Santa Barbara

Ole Helby Petersen
Roskilde University

Lena Brogaard
Roskilde University

Trevor Brown
The Ohio State University

Shaftesbury Road, Cambridge CB2 8EA, United Kingdom

One Liberty Plaza, 20th Floor, New York, NY 10006, USA

477 Williamstown Road, Port Melbourne, VIC 3207, Australia

314–321, 3rd Floor, Plot 3, Splendor Forum, Jasola District Centre, New Delhi – 110025, India

103 Penang Road, #05–06/07, Visioncrest Commercial, Singapore 238467

Cambridge University Press is part of Cambridge University Press & Assessment, a department of the University of Cambridge.

We share the University's mission to contribute to society through the pursuit of education, learning and research at the highest international levels of excellence.

www.cambridge.org
Information on this title: www.cambridge.org/9781009578622

DOI: 10.1017/9781009180771

© Matthew Potoski, Ole Helby Petersen, Lena Brogaard, and Trevor Brown 2025

This publication is in copyright. Subject to statutory exception and to the provisions of relevant collective licensing agreements, no reproduction of any part may take place without the written permission of Cambridge University Press & Assessment.

When citing this work, please include a reference to the DOI 10.1017/9781009180771

First published 2025

A catalogue record for this publication is available from the British Library

ISBN 978-1-009-57862-2 Hardback
ISBN 978-1-009-18076-4 Paperback
ISSN 2515-4303 (online)
ISSN 2515-429X (print)

Cambridge University Press & Assessment has no responsibility for the persistence or accuracy of URLs for external or third-party internet websites referred to in this publication and does not guarantee that any content on such websites is, or will remain, accurate or appropriate.

For EU product safety concerns, contact us at Calle de José Abascal, 56, 1°, 28003 Madrid, Spain, or email eugpsr@cambridge.org

Managing Public Sector Contracts

Market Frictions and Human Resources Solutions

Elements in Public and Nonprofit Administration

DOI: 10.1017/9781009180771
First published online: December 2025

Matthew Potoski
University of California, Santa Barbara

Ole Helby Petersen
Roskilde University

Lena Brogaard
Roskilde University

Trevor Brown
The Ohio State University

Author for correspondence: Matthew Potoski, mpotoski@bren.ucsb.edu

Abstract: This Element presents a framework for analyzing the complexities of contracting, how these vary across circumstances, the ways contract managers can address challenges, and the skills of contract managers. The framework is grounded on central concepts. Market frictions are underlying imperfections that cause common contracting problems; contract management activities are the tasks and procedures that contract managers perform to prepare and execute the purchase; and skills are the ability to perform contract management activities that identify and mitigate frictions. These concepts are interdependent – market frictions can influence the efficacy of contract management activities, activities may reduce or increase the presence of frictions, and skills may influence both the choice and effectiveness of activities in addressing contracting challenges. Omitting any of these components is likely to result in misleading accounts of the root causes and potential solutions to contracting challenges.

Keywords: government contracting, human resources, market frictions, public management, contracting

© Matthew Potoski, Ole Helby Petersen, Lena Brogaard, and Trevor Brown 2025

ISBNs: 9781009578622 (HB), 9781009180764 (PB), 9781009180771 (OC)
ISSNs: 2515-4303 (online), 2515-429X (print)

Contents

1 Introduction   1

2 Contracts, Contract Management, and Public Values   6

3 Market Frictions as a Source of Contracting Challenges   14

4 Contract Management Skills for Market Frictions   33

5 The Framework Applied: Diagnosing and Treating Quality Shading   51

6 Conclusion   62

References   68

1 Introduction

Citizens and academic scholars both tend to evaluate governments through the services they provide, such as education, public safety, transport systems, and social welfare programs. Of course, governments do not always produce these services through their own agencies and employees – they often purchase them from third parties.[1] Governments buy buildings, supplies, and equipment. They contract out for services of all types, including legal advice, health care, employment programs, and road repairs. In some circumstances, governments may have no choice but to purchase items like fighter jets or complex IT systems. Today, purchasing constitutes a significant part of how governments around the world provide goods and services to their citizenry. Among the OECD countries, government purchasing accounts for around 13 percent of national GDP and around 27 percent of total government expenditures (OECD 2023, pp. 120–121). This has made government purchasing a central focus in public management research and practice (Johnston and Girth 2012; Brunjes 2022; Dimand et al. 2023a; Piatak and Jensen 2024).

The promise of effective contracting is based on a premise so simple that it often goes unspoken: The exchange of resources between a government buyer and a private seller leaves each party better off, as suggested by Adam Smith's hidden hand metaphor (Smith 2000). Private sellers may be able to produce products more efficiently, perhaps due to their focused expertise, specialized processes, and scale economies (Domberger and Jensen 1997; Bennmarker et al. 2013). Market competition provides incentives for them to offer higher-quality products at lower prices, lest they lose out on sales to other sellers (Savas 1987; Domberger and Jensen 1997; Andersson and Jordahl 2011). Effective government purchasing can free resources for other goals. The government receives a product that is more valuable to them than the costs of acquiring it while the seller receives compensation that is greater than the cost to produce the product and bring it to the market. When markets work in this way, purchasing creates win–win outcomes for government buyers and private sellers.

---

[1] Government purchases come in many forms (Savas 1987; Domberger and Jensen 1997; Andersson and Jordahl 2011). Governments can buy directly from vendors through market transactions. Other means of exchange include vouchers, franchises, public–private partnerships, social impact bonds, and privatization through divestment of public assets. These vehicles of exchange between governments and markets share common features. In all of them, the government and private vendor exchange resource and the government financially compensates the vendor for delivering a service, product, or solving other tasks (Domberger and Jensen 1997). All these exchanges also occur through a contract or similar arrangement between the buyer and the seller. We use the terms purchasing and contracting to refer to when the government provides financial value in return for goods and services. Other terms in the literature include acquisition, procurement, outsourcing, and privatization.

However, government purchasing too often does not work in this idealized way (Shaoul, Stafford, and Stapleton 2006; Bel, Fageda, and Warner 2010; Hansen, Petersen, and Bel 2023). There are many ways in which contracts can fail to deliver value, perhaps most notably when the exchange leaves the government worse off than before the purchase. Media reports provide plenty of examples. In 2018, the Danish Defense launched Denmark's largest-ever contract, an endeavor to purchase cleaning, catering, and ground maintenance for the county's military. While the goals were to cut costs by 30 percent and improve service quality, in the first year of the contract military personnel submitted 3,300 complaints for unclean barracks and soldiers not receiving recommended daily minimum nutrition (Olesen and Junker 2022). The contract was terminated with a penalty to the private seller and additional public expenses for hiring more service personnel. Other times, government purchases deliver less value than anticipated. For instance, contracts for construction of sixteen large hospitals in Denmark faced significant budget overruns, resulting in a reduction in bed capacity, treatment rooms, and removal of entire floors (Danish National Audit 2020). In some of the projects, water leaked through the roof, while others remained unfinished more than five years after the deadline (Langemark and Midtiby 2024).

How to improve contract outcomes through better preparation and execution of the exchange has been extensively scrutinized in public management research (Kelman 1990; Kettl 2010; Brown, Potoski, and Van Slyke 2018; Anguelov 2020; Casady, Petersen, and Brogaard 2023). For contracting to produce value, governments need to be "smart" buyers and implement management steps that effectively address contracting challenges (Jørgensen and Bozeman 2002). One prescription from this literature is for the government to engage in management activities that ensure contracting yields more value, such as defining purchasing needs, writing detailed contracts, and monitoring product quality (Cooper 2002). Another prescription is for the managers to build a cooperative relationship between the buyer and the seller in which both pursue shared value through trust and reciprocity (Poppo and Zenger 2002; Van Slyke 2007; Lamothe and Lamothe 2012; Frydlinger, Hart, and Vitasek 2019; Domingos et al. 2025). An implication of prescriptions such as these is that problematic contracting outcomes arise from the absence of contract management activities: The contract was not written with sufficient precision, or the relationship lacked enough trust.

Defining the contract management challenge as merely implementing activities or building relationships belies contracting's underlying complexity and what needs to be done to improve contract outcomes. A first complexity is that the circumstances of contracting vary in important ways. The "smart" steps for purchasing paper clips must surely be different than those for buying eldercare services. How can managers diagnose contracting circumstances and identify the management activities that fit them? A second complexity is that contract management is a human activity, performed by people who can bring more or less skill and ability to the task. Contract management performed with more skill is likely to improve the outcomes. A third complexity is that the factors that independently influence contracting outcomes also have causal relationships among each other. Contract management can change the circumstances of the exchange, perhaps reducing the circumstances that caused the problem in the first place. Moreover, when people engage in contract management to address the circumstances of an exchange, they may improve their skills in contract management. A final complexity is that the effects of circumstances, contract management activities, and skills, can depend on the level of the other factors. The effectiveness of contract management activities may be low with less skilled staff but high with more skilled staff; likewise, purchasing skills may be less important for relatively simple tasks like buying paper clips but crucial for complex purchases of military hardware.

This Element presents a framework for identifying contracting challenges and the ways government contract management can address them. The framework provides an analytic lens that reveals the complexities of contracting challenges and how they vary across circumstances, the different ways contract managers can address the challenges, and the skills that fit different contracting circumstances and management activities. We begin our presentation by introducing the framework's three central concepts: market frictions, contract management activities, and skills. Market frictions are underlying market imperfections that cause common contracting problems; contract management activities are the tasks and procedures that contract managers perform to prepare and execute the purchase; and skills are the ability to perform contract management activities to identify and mitigate frictions. All three concepts are interdependent – market frictions can influence the efficacy of contract management activities, activities may reduce or increase the presence of frictions, and skills may influence both the choice and effectiveness of activities in addressing contracting challenges. Scholarly analyses of contracting must therefore account for all three concepts and their interdependencies. Omitting any one of these components is likely to result in an incomplete or even misleading account of the root causes and potential solutions to contracting challenges. In the following paragraphs, we briefly introduce our framework – market frictions, contract management activities, and skills – as a conceptual lens for diagnosing and treating contracting problems and analyzing the complexities among them.

The framework begins with *market frictions* as the foundation for diagnosing the conditions that create contracting challenges. A market friction is a deviation from the ideal (but rarely present) conditions required for maximally efficient market transactions. Market frictions exist, for example, when the buyer and seller have less than full information about the exchange, and when property rights do not specify all of the buyer and seller's rights and obligations (Mahoney and Qian 2013). Market frictions vary in both scope and severity across different purchasing scenarios, and most exchanges are characterized by multiple frictions appearing at the same time. Market frictions result in contracting challenges and offer an explanation for how the value of government contracting can vary across circumstances and products. A diagnosis of contracting problems must therefore start with an account of the root causes of contracting challenges – the frictions and combinations of frictions that characterize each exchange. The framework facilitates theoretically informed diagnoses of how the challenges of government contracting can vary across circumstances and products while also providing insight into the appropriate contract management practices in response.

Markets and frictions, of course, do not exist independently of *contract management activities*. Public sector contract management is the set of activities government buyers perform to make the purchase happen and obtain value from the contract. Contract management includes analyzing needs; writing, negotiating, and signing contracts; monitoring supplier performance; and bringing the contract to completion. Contracting challenges and the management activities for addressing them can be different for different types of products and circumstances. Effective contract management needs to assess market frictions and then deploy management activities that address the friction or mitigate its consequence using two common approaches: formal and relational contract management. To address the cause of incomplete information, for example, a buyer might invest in market search to determine which product will best suit its needs. Alternatively, the buyer might design a contract that requires the seller to improve the product if it does not adequately fit the purchase need. This example illustrates an important point we return to Section 3.3: Different contract management activities mitigate the same market friction, sometimes even with the same cost–benefit value.

Just as frictions are the underlying source of contracting challenges, they also help identify the *contract skills* needed to perform contract management activities effectively. In our framework, a skill is the ability to perform contract management activities to diagnose or treat a market friction. For example, the skill of contract writing is determining whether expending resources to write a detailed contract effectively addresses the underlying friction and then drafting the contract to mitigate its root cause. Contract skills are important for analyzing market frictions and providing a precise diagnosis of the problem and thus identify the appropriate management activities that can effectively address it. If the underlying cause of a failed purchase is that the government buyer did not have sufficient information to describe the need for the purchase, writing a more detailed contract will not fix the problem. Other skills – such as information acquisition and market management – might help mitigate the cause of the market friction. A skilled contract manager may acquire relevant information to better specify the purchasing need and write the contract. Finally, skills can help mitigate the consequences of market frictions. When faced with a complex purchase where the contract is likely to be highly incomplete, a contract manager may deploy skills to write a flexible contract and build a relationship that enlists the seller in defining the problem and aligns the parties' interests throughout the contract.

Analyzing government contracting through the lens of market frictions identifies the circumstances that create contracting challenges, the management activities that can address the frictions' causes and consequences, and the skills that allow contract managers to perform these activities. Examining these three components together reveals how market frictions create the need for contract management activities and skills. At the same time, contract management activities can either reduce or exacerbate market frictions while also developing skills through experience and practice. Skills, in turn, may influence both market frictions and the choice of contract management activities. For instance, the framework suggests that an incomplete information problem might be addressed by improving contract manager's skills in information acquisition or by requiring sellers to disclose relevant information in the contract process. In addition, the effective contract management activities for a specific purchase depends, at least in part, on the level of skills possessed by the government. Our framework facilitates analyses of how different types of skills and variations in skill levels affect the implementation and success of contract management activities. For example, managers more skilled in contract monitoring may be more likely to effectively evaluate product quality than less skilled managers. The framework thus facilitates analysis of market frictions, contract management activities, and skills present in each circumstance. By adopting this framework, public management researchers gain a powerful tool to analyze government contracting with greater precision and relevance.

Our framework offers several contributions to the public management field. We show how economic theories of markets can be integrated with public management theories to identify contract management solutions that harness public value. Our framework also connects contract management with theories of human resource management. Combining these perspectives integrates the "human skills" dimension often overlooked in the public sector contracting literature, thereby advancing the contracting literature by identifying human resources that can improve outcomes. The framework facilitates both descriptive and prescriptive analysis. Descriptive analysis with our framework can retrospectively examine contracting scenarios to identify why outcomes occurred, while also revealing how frictions in a scenario both causes the outcome and is influenced by management activities and the skills of those performing them. Without our framework, a descriptive analysis of the contracting scenario could misidentify the cause of contract outcomes. Prescriptive analysis with our framework can prospectively identify leverage points that would likely change (or improve) contract outcomes, while also helping scholars and practitioners understand that the effectiveness of choosing (or changing) a contract management activity depends on the nature of the frictions and the skills of those involved. Taken together, our framework facilitates scholarly analyses of the interplay between market frictions, contract management activities, and skills, and helps practitioners in deploying management strategies and human resources that address contracting challenges to harness public value.

This Element is structured into five sections in addition to this introduction. In Section 2, we begin by laying out concepts that are central to scholarly analysis of government purchasing: contracts, contract management activities, and public values and costs at stake. Then, in Section 3, we outline the assumptions of perfectly functioning markets before examining common market frictions that deviate from these ideals in government contracting. We also identify two fundamental contract management approaches that can be employed to counter these market frictions: formal and relational contracting. Next, in Section 4, we present a set of human skills that contract managers can use to diagnose and treat market frictions to deliver public value in government contracting. Then, in Section 5, we summarize our framework and apply it to a common contracting challenge – quality shading – where multiple market frictions, contract management activities, and skills interact. Finally, in Section 6, we conclude this Element by summarizing how our framework facilitates analysis of government contracting challenges and solutions as well as discussing implications for research and practice.

2 Contracts, Contract Management, and Public Values

The aim of government contracting is to acquire value greater than the cost of obtaining the product (Jørgensen and Bozeman 2002). The value proposition of government contracting is often more complex than that of private sector contracting because of the many dimensions of value and the wide range of stakeholders involved. The value produced by a government contract can, of course, affect the purchasing organization itself: A poorly performing contract may result in missing products or reduced budgets. In private contracting, outcomes also matter to owners and shareholders. However, because government buyers serve the public, the range of stakeholders is often broader, and can include clients, taxpayers, politicians, and the general citizenry (Amirkhanyan et al. 2019; Piatak and Jensen 2024). Likewise, the value outcomes in government contracting may also be broader than in private contracting. As we discuss in Section 2.3, the value in government contracting can relate not only to the immediate performance of the product in use but also to broader considerations such as transparency, fairness, environmental consequences, and equity (Dimand et al. 2023b; Brunjes and Rodriguez-Plesa 2024).

Market exchanges require rules, manifested in public law provisions and contracts, that specify the buyer and seller's rights and obligations and the procedures through which the parties will exchange resources for mutual gain. No exchanges magically appear without human agency. Public procurement regulations require governments to follow a series of steps before awarding a contract (Tadelis 2012). To make the exchange happen, a government buyer must actively define their needs, search for suppliers, negotiate contract terms, and monitor contract compliance (Amirkhanyan, Kim, and Lambright 2010; Anguelov 2020), while the seller takes their own similar steps to win and execute the contract (Petersen, Potoski, and Brown 2022). Finally, and perhaps most importantly, in government contracting, the costs and benefits of contracting extend well beyond the purchase price and the direct benefits of the product's performance. Identifying these costs and values, and the trade-offs among them, is complex (Bozeman 2002; Piatak and Jensen 2024). For a contract to be successful, the public value derived from the product must exceed the costs of purchasing.

In this section, we introduce important contracting concepts. Analyses of government purchasing need to consider the contract, contract management activities, and public values and costs at stake in the purchase. Indeed, most scholarly analyses of government contracting begin – and sometimes end – with these core concepts. We start in Section 2.1 with an introduction to the core of the exchange: the contract itself and a series of essential contract management activities that governments often perform to prepare and execute the exchange. Next, in Section 2.2, we introduce three groups of contract terms that can aid governments in realizing the potential of market exchange: product rules, exchange rules, and governance rules. Then, having established these core terms, in Section 2.3, we focus on the goals that government contracting is ultimately about: producing product value and social and process values at a reasonable cost. We also discuss trade-offs between public values, costs, and risk. Finally, in Section 2.4, we show that contract analyses need to expand beyond these concepts to include factors such as characteristics of the product and the circumstances of the exchange.

2.1 Contracts and Contract Management Activities

A contract is the legally binding rights and obligations that govern the relationship between buyers and sellers (Tirole 1999; Hart and Moore 2008, p. 1). Some of these obligations and rights are defined in public law: Bribery and false advertising are illegal, as is refusing to pay for a product once it has been received. Beyond public law, contracts can include terms that are the products of negotiations between the government buyer and private seller and can be enforced in the legal system. Negotiated terms can include the product's price, quantity, and quality; how it will be delivered; how the product's quality will be verified; and how disputes between the government and the seller will be resolved. Sometimes these negotiated terms are formally inscribed in written contracts (Tirole 1999; Brown, Potoski, and Van Slyke 2016). Other times, the terms are more informal, perhaps as simple verbal agreements, which may be more difficult to enforce through legal channels. A seller may, for example, make a verbal promise to extend the product warranty or perform additional maintenance not specified in the written contract.

The terms of a contract define the aspirations of the exchange, what the buyer and seller should do for each to gain value, and how the parties will communicate and resolve disputes in the contract period. Aspirations, of course, are not always reality. A contract requires action by the buyer and seller to ensure the exchange of resources takes place. Contract management brings the legal foundation of the contract to life in activities governments perform to execute the exchange.

Much of the corpus of scholarly advice for public managers presents contract management as a sequence of decisions (Warren 2014; Van Weele 2018) – the initiation of the contract oftentimes referred to as ex ante contract management activities, and the execution of the contract often referred to as ex post contract management activities (Dyer and Chu 2003).[2] In the ex ante phase, the job of the government contract manager is to define the problem the purchase needs to address and the type of products that can be purchased to address those needs.

---

[2] Before writing the requirement specification, government buyers sometimes conduct analyses to determine whether a task should be carried out in-house or purchased from the market. These "make-or-buy" analyses (Brown and Potoski 2003; Levin and Tadelis 2010; Hefetz and Warner 2012) are particularly relevant when contracting for services that the government could potentially deliver using its own employees. In contrast, they are less relevant when contracting for goods or public works projects, which governments typically cannot execute themselves. The make-or-buy analysis takes place prior to the start of the purchasing process and is therefore not included in Figure 1. Nonetheless, it is a key public management activity for assessing whether to initiate the purchase process or to produce using government personnel.

The contract management activities include identifying needs, specifying product requirements, establishing selection processes (e.g., open, restricted, or negotiated procedures), determining payment schemes (e.g., cost reimbursement or fixed price), and publicizing the request for proposals (Petersen et al. 2019). Next, contract award activities include evaluating bids, selecting a vendor, negotiating contract terms, and any additional procedures for the exchange (Amirkhanyan, Kim, and Lambright 2010). The formal award to the selected seller and signing of the contract close the ex ante phase.

In the ex post phase, the buyer and seller usually conduct start-up meetings, the seller delivers the product, and the government buyer monitors the seller's performance and assesses whether it has received the agreed-upon product. Government buyers then determine whether to close-out the contract with full payment, terminate the contract without full payment if dissatisfied with the product and potentially enter legal proceedings, or renegotiate, renew, or extend the contract. The ex post phase lasts throughout the entire contract period – unless the contract is terminated prematurely for convenience, material breach, or other reasons (Brunjes 2022, p. 85). The main steps and activities of the government contract management process are summarized in Figure 1.

Listing these activities as a sequence of steps risks the impression that every purchase occurs with some standardized set of activities. This is true in a broad and general sense: Every purchase begins with some definition of what needs to be purchased and ends with payment, termination, or renewal. Of course, these activities oftentimes vary in important ways across real-world purchases. Writing requirement specifications and negotiating contract terms for buying office supplies is very different than defining needs and negotiating contract terms for buying mental health services. In addition, the effectiveness of contract management activities depends on the public value objectives the government pursues, which we return to in Section 2.3.

2.2 Contract Terms: Product, Exchange, and Governance Rules

Having established the main steps and activities of government contract management, we can now take a closer look at the terms of the contract. Whether

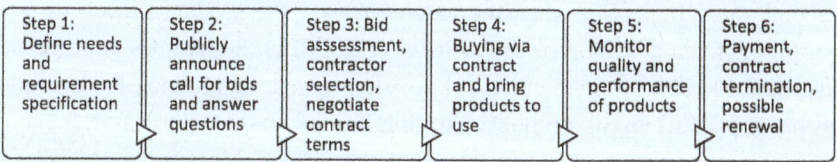

Figure 1 The steps and main activities of government contract management.
Source: Authors' compilation.

based in public law or negotiated between the buyer and the seller, the contract terms can be viewed in three groups: *product rules* for quality, functions, quantity, and other properties of the product; *exchange rules* for how product will be delivered and how the seller will be compensated; and *governance rules* for verifying that both parties have abided by the contract and defines principles for adjudicating disputes (Brown, Potoski, and Van Slyke 2016). We discuss these three types of contracts terms in the remainder of this section.

The first set of terms – product rules – defines the qualities, features, quantities, and functions of the product, which in contract management parlance are sometimes referred to as requirements definition (Warren 2014). The purpose of the requirements definition is to describe – before the purchase is completed – the qualities, functions, and performance the buyer wants the seller to deliver. For example, defining fabric quality for hospital uniforms determines their comfort and durability, and descriptions of procedures a cleaning provider must perform determine the level of cleanliness. In addition, the requirements can also support social values such as requiring that cotton must be organic and must be produced with fair labor practices.

The second set of contract terms – exchange rules – specify what the government and the seller need to do when executing the exchange. Exchange rules can specify when and where the product is to be delivered, the price of the product, and the payment conditions. The terms may also specify how the seller must rectify errors and defects in the product. Each of these exchange rules can be designed in different ways. In a fixed price contract, the government pays for product qualities or outcomes. In a cost-reimbursement contract, the government pays for inputs, such as hours of work the seller provides (Kim and Brown 2012; Brown, Kim, and Roberts 2015). For product delivery, the contract may specify that the product must be delivered on a specific date (e.g., when the local emergency service buys five new fire trucks) or must be delivered on an ongoing basis (e.g., as part of a framework contract for office equipment).

The third set of contract terms – governance rules – specifies decision-making, monitoring and enforcement, and dispute resolution provisions. Decision-making procedures describe how the two parties will make decisions throughout the production and delivery of the product. Governance terms become more important when the requirements – the product rules – cannot be fully defined at the outset (Frydlinger et al. 2021). Sometimes governance rules allow sellers to make unilateral decisions about the product, for example changing product inputs, without consulting the government purchaser. In other cases, input changes may require government approval. Monitoring procedures define how buying governments assess whether the seller has produced the product quality, inputs, and outcomes specified in the contract (Brown and

Potoski 2006; Anguelov 2020). The governance terms can also specify which sanctions the government can impose if the seller does not comply with the contract terms, such as daily fines for late delivery of a construction project. Finally, the governance terms can also contain provisions for contract amendments and dispute resolution procedures.

These three types of contract terms exist both in their own right and through their interaction to support the objectives of the contract. Government buyers may, for example, specify highly detailed product and exchange terms while leaving governance terms to general public law provisions, such as resolving disputes through the courts. Alternatively, they may define more open-ended product and exchange rules and scaffold the contract with more extensive governance terms (Frydlinger et al. 2021). Ideally, government buyers select the combination of terms that delivers the greatest public value at the lowest possible cost. We now turn to public value, costs, and the trade-offs among them in government contracting.

2.3 Public Value and Costs in Government Contracting

Like other public programs, government contracts implement public policies. Thus, understanding the effectiveness of contract management requires analysis of the value and costs across at stake in different contracting scenarios. Government contracting involves complex trade-offs between public value and costs across many different stakeholders (Jørgensen and Bozeman 2002; Malacina et al. 2022). The most obvious contracting cost is the purchase price, while the public value accrues from how the product contributes to government goals. There are also less obvious costs and values, such as the risk that the product's quality or performance will be lower than anticipated, the time and energy spent making the purchase, and whether the item was produced in ways that align with politically mandated social and process values. Assessing how well contracting works requires precise accounting of these different costs and dimensions of public value. In this section, we briefly present key terms for assessing public value and costs in government contracting, drawing on the literature on public value (Moore 1994; Andersen et al. 2012; Bryson, Crosby, and Bloomberg 2014).

When a government makes a purchase, it can receive several types of value from both the product itself and the process of buying it. A product's *functional quality* is the amount of value it contributes toward the problem the government sought to address through the purchase. A senior citizens' agency may need a high-quality walker to support its elderly clientele, and the military may need superior fighter jets to keep the country safe. Beyond these direct functional qualities, governments also look to pursue *social value* through their purchases (Dimand et al. 2023b; Brunjes and Rodriguez-Plesa 2024). Social value refers to qualities not directly related to the product's immediate use but is important because of political mandates and/or the sentiments of clients, taxpayers, and citizenry the government serves (Piatak and Jensen 2024). A government may want to purchase walkers and fighter jets that were produced in socially responsible ways, such as environment-friendly practices or with wages above the legal minimum. The public value a government receives from a purchase reflects both the functional quality of the product and its contribution to social value.

In addition, governments may pursue process value through the process of making the purchase. *Process value* is not directly related to how well a product functions or how it was produced, but to how the product is acquired. Process values include requirements to openly announce calls for bids, publish the evaluation criteria in advance of contract award, and require transparency and written documentation in all phases of the process. Many countries have regulations that codify contracting processes (such as the Federal Procurement Act or the European Union Procurement Directives) to ensure process value in public purchasing, such as transparency, open access to bidding, and equal treatment of businesses (Van Weele 2018). These government procurement procedures and other regulations (such as the Freedom of Information Act) may both generate public value and be a source of greater frictions in government-to-business than in business-to-business contracting (Tadelis 2012; Potoski, Petersen, and Brown 2023).

Just as a product can provide different types of public value, it can also have different types of costs. The most obvious cost is the *purchase price* the government pays for obtaining ownership rights to the product, which is equivalent to the sticker price a consumer pays in a supermarket. In addition, the cost of a product also includes transaction cost expenditures to prepare and execute the exchange, such as the costs of analyzing needs, writing product specifications, negotiating contracts, and monitoring product quality (Williamson 1979, 1996; Dyer and Chu 2003; David and Han 2004). Another cost of the purchase is risk: As the purchase unfolds, the government may end up paying more or receiving lower quality than it initially anticipated.[3] Finally, a product can have ownership costs, such as the cost of storage, maintenance, use, and disposal. Minimizing the total purchase and ownership costs enables governments to free up resources for other activities of value to the citizenry.

---

[3] The cost of risk can formally be defined as the cost deviation from some mean cost resulting from an event multiplied by the probability of the event occurring.

Table 1 summarizes these dimensions of public values and costs in government contracting.

Our discussion facilitates analytic attention to a range of trade-offs between public values and costs in contracting. First, managing government contracts means engaging trade-offs between purchase costs, functional value, and process value. When a government purchases a police car, all else being equal, it spends taxpayers' money wisely by minimizing the costs it pays to gain ownership of the car. However, the government may also decide to purchase a police car with higher quality in use, such as more safety features or a stronger engine, and thereby accept to pay a higher purchase price for a higher-quality product. Second, the government may also use contracting to pursue social value, such as buying electric cars with a lower CO_2 footprint. Buying products that align with social values may involve important trade-offs vis-à-vis purchasing costs (an electric car is often more expensive) and potentially reduced functional value because police officers would need to spend time charging the car (and thus have less time for keeping the public safe). Third, governments

Table 1 Public value and costs in government contracting

Value	Examples

Public value	• Functional value: value of the product in use (quality, performance)
	• Social value: value based on political and/or societal concerns, but not directly related to the product's immediate function (e.g., no child labor, reduction of CO_2 emission, and buying locally)
	• Process value: value derived from how the purchase is executed is important because of political mandate and/or stakeholders, but not directly related to the product itself
	  (a) Vendor rights: equal treatment, transparency (call for bids and documentation of award decision), proportionality
	  (b) The public: freedom of information, documentation of steps, and procedures

Costs	• Risk of deficiencies in public value: potential reduction in value due to functional, social, or process shortcomings or failures • Purchase price: acquisition price, costs of use, maintenance costs, residual product value at contract expiration • Transaction cost expenditures: time and money spent to prepare and execute the purchase (ex ante and ex post) • Ownership costs: costs of operation, maintenance, and disposal • Risk of cost deficiencies: potential additional costs due to shortcomings or failures

Source: Authors' compilation.

may trade off purchase costs and product quality against process value, for example when spending time and money preparing and executing a purchase according to public procurement regulations when the government already had a clear idea of the product it wanted to purchase.

2.4 Section Summary

In this section, we described contract management activities buyers can execute across the phases of contracting and defined contracts as product, exchange, and governance rules. We have also presented public value and costs that are important in assessing the outcomes of government contracting. Some of the value from contracting is related to how well the product functions in use. Other types of social and process value are not directly related to a product's immediate use but are important due to political mandates or because public procurement laws require purchases to follow specific procedures. Just like public value, contracting costs also have several dimensions – the purchase price, transaction costs, ownership costs, costs of use, and maintenance costs. We also discussed why the value proposition of government purchasing is oftentimes complicated by the fact that governments pursue many different types of value with a range of trade-offs between them.

There is a risk in discussing the values and trade-offs of contract management activities without addressing the context and circumstances in which they are deployed. Contract management activities have costs, benefits, and trade-offs among them depending on what is being purchased and the circumstances in which the purchase occurs. Some of these differences are obvious: Governments do not purchase pencils using the same methods they apply to procure complex social services. Some markets have many buyers and sellers, whereas others have few; and some exchanges require up-front investment in machinery or human competencies, whereas others do not. Circumstances can also be complex and nuanced in ways that can be difficult to diagnose and manage. The effectiveness of contract management activities depends on the fit with the contracting circumstances. Analyzing contract management needs a way to identify these circumstances, their challenges, and how management activities may alter the value from the exchange. The next step in our framework is to develop an overview of market frictions that threaten contracting's potential to deliver public value.

3 Market Frictions as a Source of Contracting Challenges

Government purchasing takes place in many different circumstances. A government may buy simple commodities, like basic foods or office supplies, with many competitors offering products in response to a well-defined need.

However, the same government also buys products under circumstances where its needs are not so clearly defined, few sellers offer potential products, and the government may struggle to evaluate the product's quality before and even after the purchase. Different circumstances lead to different contracting challenges, and the value returned from different contract management activities depends on their fit with contracting challenges. Effectively analyzing contracting therefore requires a way of categorizing circumstances and the contracting challenges that arise from them. The field of economics identifies the ideal circumstances that allow buyers and sellers to receive value from the exchange, while using the term "market failure" to describe the conditions that fall short of these ideals. In this Element, instead of "market failure," we refer to deviations from these ideal market conditions as "market frictions" (Mahoney and Qian 2013). The term "friction" suggests that these obstacles are a matter of degree; they can be stronger or weaker in different circumstances and can appear in complex combinations.

While market frictions are important, there are other reasons why government purchasing may fail to deliver value. One such reason is some form of government failure (Williams and Coase 1964; Datta-Chaudhuri 1990; Stiglitz 2010). Government failure can result from principal-agent problems, such as when the executive branch does not follow legislative prescriptions, a government agency is captured by narrow interests, or a public manager engages in corruption. Government failure can reduce the value from contracts in various ways. For example, a corrupt contract manager may take side payments from a vendor selling inferior products, or an agency may purchase services that differ from what was legislatively authorized. Another instance of government failure arises when a court does not enforce a contract. Failure can also occur within a firm, such as when a firm manager embezzles funds that were intended for the government's product. While such sources of contract failure merit inquiry, they require a deeper analysis than what can be accomplished in this Element. We assume that governments and firms function well in order to focus on interactions between the government managers and the firms selling products to governments.

We begin Section 3.1 by briefly presenting an overview of the assumptions of perfectly functioning markets: full information, complete markets, and independence of production and consumption (Mahoney and Qian 2013, p. 1021). Then, in Section 3.2, we discuss market frictions as the sources of the challenges that contract management needs to address. When presented as platonic ideals of perfection, the conditions for market exchanges are often so strict that they are rarely fully realized in real-world settings. Buyers and sellers never have perfect information, and there are always costs to negotiate and execute an exchange. For each market friction, we discuss circumstances where the friction is more likely to appear in government contracting and how these frictions are often larger and more common. The framework suggests that market conditions are not simply imposed on buyers and sellers but can also be influenced by activities that people perform. Contract management can mitigate the causes and consequences of market frictions in ways that affect contract outcomes. After reviewing the market frictions, Section 3.3 focuses on two fundamental management approaches that governments can adopt in response: formal and relational contracting. Finally, Section 3.4 summarizes this section.

3.1 Ideal Market Conditions

Economic theories of markets propose that under ideal conditions exchanges will produce Pareto-optimal welfare outcomes (Arrow and Hahn 1971; Stiglitz and Rosengaard 2015). This proposition is based on Adam Smith's notion of the invisible hand, where market competition ensures a perfect balance between supply and demand (Smith 1776). The ideal conditions are complete markets (i.e., a large number of buyers and sellers), with complete information (i.e., no imperfect and asymmetric information), and independence in production and consumption (i.e., no spillovers and externalities). Table 2 lists the ideal market conditions – complete markets, perfectly fungible assets, perfect information, perfectly defined property rights, independence in consumption and production, and zero transaction costs – and offers a brief definition for each.

Even a quick read of these conditions of ideal markets reveals how rare, if not impossible, it is to encounter these conditions in real-world exchanges. Buyers and sellers cannot conduct a purchase or sale without expending resources to advertise for exchange partners, negotiate exchange terms, and write a contract. Buyers rarely have access to the full range of information about the quality and price features of products offered by sellers in the market, not to mention the current and future behavior of these sellers. Similarly, sellers rarely have knowledge of the buyer's utility function and willingness to pay at different quality levels of the product. In addition, many markets are characterized by few buyers or sellers (Girth et al. 2012), falling far short of the ideal of perfect markets, and entering and leaving a market is rarely cost-free.

3.2 Market Frictions and Government Contracting

A market friction occurs when exchange conditions deviate from the theoretical ideal conditions of market exchange. Understanding the ideal conditions reveals that any purchase occurs under the presence of some level of market frictions. Sometimes a friction might be trivially small and have effects that participants

Table 2 Ideal market conditions

Condition	Definition
Complete markets	A competitive market with multiple buyers and sellers that can easily enter and exit the market, and all sellers are price takers
Perfectly fungible assets	A perfectly fungible asset can be interchanged at no cost with another similar asset that offers the same value or performs the same functions
Perfect information	Buyers and sellers know all that is relevant to their decisions in the exchange both now and in the future
Perfectly defined property rights	The rules of ownership and transfer are complete for all products and circumstances
Independence in consumption and production	Absence of externalities, that is, negative or positive effects not covered by the market price
Zero transaction costs	Buyers and sellers exchange products without expending any costs, such as searching for buyers and sellers

Source: Authors' compilation, with inspiration from Mahoney and Qian (2013).

do not even notice. Even small frictions may undermine the value generated from an exchange regardless of whether the exchange generates value overall. Other times, frictions can be quite large, perhaps so large that the buyer and seller are each worse off than they were before the exchange began. Frictions and their consequences may also appear differently for the buyer and the seller. For example, a buyer may have important information that the seller lacks, or a contract may require asset-specific investments only from the buyer and not from the seller.

In this section, we will discuss how common market frictions appear and how they can undermine the value buyers and sellers receive from exchanges. Examining markets through the framework helps diagnose the underlying cause of purchasing challenges and identify the potential solutions. Analyzing government contracting through the lens of market frictions offers several advantages. First, frictions may prevent exchanges from occurring even when both the buyer and seller would have been better off had the exchange happened. Reducing frictions can allow more win–win exchanges to occur. Second, frictions require the buyer and seller to spend additional resources to make the exchange happen, thereby reducing the gains realized from the exchange. Finally, market frictions increase the risk that an exchange will fail. Failure means that the buyer, seller, or both experience losses greater than the value received from the exchange. Our framework thereby provides a broader perspective on the type of costs or losses that occur in government contracting as a result of market frictions.

3.2.1 Incomplete Markets

Markets are complete when there is a sufficiently large number of buyers and sellers for every combination of product qualities so that no seller or buyer can influence prices (Stiglitz and Rosenbaum 2015). Competition among sellers drives down prices and buyers can facilitate comparisons to analyze quality/price trade-offs. In such circumstances, buyers can find a product that best fits their needs at the lowest possible price, and sellers can find buyers for what they are offering. Markets can be competitive with just a few buyers and sellers, perhaps as few as three or four of each (Smith 1962). Just as importantly, a credible threat of competition – a competitor can enter the market at trivial cost – can discipline a seller and prevent them from increasing prices arbitrarily.

There are many sources that lead to markets with no or low competition. One way is when a seller has exclusive access to valuable resources (Barney 1991) – the company can acquire some resource that increases product quality or lowers costs, and this resource is not available to competitors. Such resources can include specialized skills that lower a seller's production costs, such as unique production expertise (Pralahad and Hamel 2009), or physical factors such as proximity to customers or distribution centers. Markets can also have lower competition because of the effects of public policies and government regulations. Some regulations reduce competition by placing explicit restrictions on who is permitted to sell products and others limit the number of sellers by requiring sellers to obtain a license or certification to be eligible to sell in a market. Intellectual property rights, such as patents and copyrights, grant the owner monopoly control of the sale and distribution of ideas. Public policies can also restrict market competition even if they do not explicitly prescribe who can sell particular products. Complex regulation in an industry can also shelter incumbent firms from competition. Each regulation requires a new company in a market to make up-front investments to understand how requirements apply to them.

Another form of limited competition can occur when the buyer makes costly investments to purchase the first of a series of products; the buyer can be beholden to a single seller if the investment loses value when switching to another seller. Noncompetitive markets, sometimes called "thin markets," occur when there are so few sellers that those in the market no longer have to compete by offering higher-quality products or more favorable prices and contract terms.[4] An extreme version of noncompetitive markets is a monopoly, where a single seller achieves market power to increase prices or reduces supply – both of which raise the seller's profits while making buyers worse off. When a monopolist reduces supply or raises prices, buyers who would have benefited from a purchase at the competitive market price end up not finding the combination of price and quality they are willing to purchase.

A product's fixed and marginal production costs can lead to natural monopoly. The term "natural monopoly" is used to describe products with very high fixed costs and very low marginal costs. When production has low fixed costs relative to marginal costs, there are small returns to scale. Larger companies selling more products in volume have the same costs of producing each unit as smaller companies selling fewer products. The marginal costs of production are essentially constant at all scales of production. When fixed costs relative to marginal costs are very high, there are returns to scale. Such conditions bestow a competitive advantage to large producers: Their larger scale of production leads to lower costs per unit. Without the cost advantage from large-scale production, new companies are unable to enter the market and offer prices that can compete against established incumbents.[5]

Governments often buy products in markets that are not complete. Limited competition or even monopoly markets are recurring market frictions that can impact the price, quality, and other aspects of government purchasing. When public contract managers prepare to make a purchase, they typically evaluate the sellers and the products they are offering. Indeed, in some jurisdictions, government regulations require government managers to consider several competing bids before selecting a product to purchase. Sometimes, governments buy products such as office supplies, where competition is high, making it easier to buy at a favorable price and quality. However, just as often, governments buy products in thin markets comprising only a few sellers or even one seller (Girth

---

[4] Similar problems can occur under monopsony conditions, where a market has just a single buyer. Monopsonistic buyers can set market prices (Robinson 1934). Monopsony may be rare in consumer markets for products like milk and bread, for which there are millions of household buyers, but are more frequent for unique products for which there is limited demand (Girth et al. 2012), such as job training, street repair, and information technology systems (e.g., government tax processing and passport application systems).

[5] Not every product and market conveys advantage to the first mover. In some cases, the first seller incurs unique up-front investments that subsequent sellers do not experience. The first seller may need to spend considerable resources to design and make a product that fits the government's purchasing needs, but subsequent sellers can simply observe the product and make it at much lower costs.

et al. 2012), whether it is complex IT systems or specialized welfare services, where sellers have incentives to demand high prices and/or lower quality to increase profits at the government's expense. Or the government may be the only purchaser, such as for unique products like police cars or social services for people with special needs. Once the government makes the unique purchase, other potential sellers may face high market entry costs and struggle to offer comparable products at competitive prices.

3.2.2 Fungible Assets

A perfectly fungible asset can be easily interchanged with another similar asset that offers the same value or performs the same functions. Assets in this context have a broad definition. Assets include production equipment, such as machinery, buildings, and raw materials. Assets also include human resources like the skills and expertise of a company's workforce. Many commodities are fungible assets; a gallon of water can be replaced by any other gallon of water to accomplish the same tasks. Employees are fungible when they can change employers and produce the same value in their job. In ideal market conditions, buyers and sellers are able to replace physical and human assets at no cost.

In many real-world transactions, asset specificity constitutes an important market friction. Assets are specific (or non-fungible) if they lose value when they are put to alternative use or are acquired by a new owner. A seller can end up owning a specific asset when it customizes its production processes to meet the unique needs of a single buyer – the costs of customization are lost if the seller looks to sell to other buyers. A buyer can likewise make specific investments when making a purchase. A buyer may need to invest effort to learn how to use a unique product. If they end up buying something else, those specific investments are lost because they do not apply to their new purchase.

Investing in a specific asset can leave the buyer and seller subject to the holdup problem (Hart 2009). The holdup problem can arise when the exchange of resources occurs at different times, one party holds asset-specific resources, and the other party has the opportunity to not follow up on their end of the deal. The first mover makes an asset-specific investment for the deal, while the other party receives the return payment at a later time. A problem is that once the first mover makes the investment, the second mover has incentive to change the terms of the deal for their own gain, knowing that the first mover will lose value if the exchange does not occur. The first mover may be reluctant to make the upfront payment without assurance of payment in return.

Sometimes sellers make asset-specific investments: A seller customizing production to a single buyer faces losses when trying to sell to others. Other times, the buyer makes the asset-specific investment. For example, anticipating buying a new information technology product at an attractive price, a buyer may need to make investments prior to purchase to learn how to use the new software or hardware. The seller, recognizing the buyer's investment, may behave perfunctorily by raising prices, knowing that the buyer would lose the investment's value if it chose another information technology product to purchase. Anticipating this scenario, the buyer may not make the specific investments in the first place and look for information technology products that do not require them. Even though the buyer and seller would be better off if the exchange occurred on its original terms, the exchange does not happen.

Governments often buy unique products that no others even consider purchasing, such as aircraft carriers, unemployment software systems, or training programs for the mentally disabled. These products are often tailored to fit the government's distinct needs and require special skills for government employees to use them, which makes asset specificity a common market friction that contract managers face. Companies may look to avoid circumstances where selling requires specialized investments. Also, a seller may need to spend considerable up-front fixed costs to learn how to make a product to meet the government's needs. If a seller makes a specific investment and the buyer does not, the seller is exposed to potential holdup problems. On the other hand, sellers have incentive to engage in transactions that require buyers to make asset-specific investments, such as buying a printer that can only be used with the seller's cartridges. In such cases, buyers face costs of switching to rivals' products, thereby conferring an advantage on the seller, which can be realized as higher prices and profits.

3.2.3 Incomplete Information

Under ideal market conditions, buyers and sellers have complete information; they know all that is relevant to make decisions for the exchange. Buyers are aware of all products and their qualities and prices, how sellers will perform in an exchange, and the preferences of other buyers. Likewise, sellers know buyers' preferences for price and quality and what all other sellers in the market are offering. Perfect information makes the buyer capable of comparing and choosing the product that reflects their preferences and guides the sellers' offerings of price and quality to the buyers' needs. Incomplete information can also come in the form of events that are impossible to predict, such as extreme weather, pandemics, or natural disasters.

Rarely if ever do buyers and sellers have full information about the market, products, and all other buyers and sellers. The degree to which buyers and sellers have imperfect information is a market friction. Sellers may not be aware of buyers willing to purchase their products and may miss sales. Buyers may experience losses as well, as sellers may look to sell lower-quality products at higher prices or offer an expensive solution that exceeds the buyer's needs. If a seller offers a substandard or overpriced product, the buyer can find another seller offering a higher quality or cheaper product on more favorable terms.

Imperfect information also leads to friction when one side of the exchange has more information than the other. In a lemons market, the quality of goods ranges from low to high, and sellers know more about the quality of a good than do buyers (Akerloff 1974). Under asymmetric information, a seller might claim to have produced a quality good without having done so. A buyer may be unwilling to purchase products offered at prices indicating higher quality, fearing that the product's quality falls short of the seller's claims or that the seller may not follow through to produce the quality of service the buyer initially sought to purchase (Holmström 1979). Sellers may seek out these advantaged opportunities by pursuing markets where information problems are prominent, such as markets for products that are innovative or untested in a specific scenario.

Every market exchange occurs with incomplete information – there may be other options for purchase, products may not perform as anticipated, future conditions may require different types of products, and so on. When sellers know more about the range and quality of goods than buyers do, they have an information advantage – they can offer products of lower quality or higher price. Sometimes the challenge of imperfect information is a result of the absence of competition – there are simply too few sellers to allow comparison shopping. Other times, incomplete information stems from ambiguity about which products can best solve the problem a government seeks to address. Without information about alternatives, a purchasing government may wind up paying too much or getting too little.

Information frictions are likely to be larger in government purchasing. When government is the sole purchaser, the absence of competition limits the information about product quality and prices. Access to and analysis of information is more straightforward for government buyers in markets for simple products with high levels of competition, where sellers are motivated to share information and describing product features is easy. Another reason government purchasing occurs under larger information frictions is that government purchasing regulations often impose additional requirements on sellers and their products. Government purchasing regulations may require sustainable production methods, fair labor standards, or other product and production qualities. Purchasing any product requires market research to some degree: which sellers offer the products they wish to buy at what quality and price combinations, how will the product perform, and so on. Purchasing products under government regulations requires yet more information about product quality and production so ensure the products meet the requirements. However, even under these circumstances, incomplete and asymmetric information is a persistent market friction in government contracting, as sellers will (nearly) always know more about the products they offer and how they will behave during the contract period.

3.2.4 Property Rights

Property rights define the buyer and seller's rights and obligations in the exchange, including what the resource is, how it can be used, and how it can be transferred from one owner to another. For any market to function perfectly, the rules need to clearly and specifically define the buyer and seller's rights and obligations for all potential contingencies and circumstances (Alchian and Demsetz 1973; Fama and Jensen 1983; Hart and Moore 2007). Perfectly defined and enforced property rights facilitate exchanges by providing the buyer and seller with confidence they will receive the value they expect in the exchange, including returns on investments in the specific product and contract. When a buyer and seller agree to an exchange under perfectly defined property rights, they both have incentives to make value-enhancing investments, knowing that they will each be rewarded according to the terms of the exchange. Market transactions for groceries, for example, have relatively uniform and complete practices for property rights between buyers and sellers – for instance, a seller will often replace a bottle of milk dropped on the floor inside the store, whereas it becomes the buyer's responsibility if the same happens in the parking lot.

Incomplete property rights are a market friction because without clearly defined and enforced property rights, it is difficult to create and enforce contracts that allocate risks, rewards, and responsibilities between the buyer and the seller (Hart and Moore 2007). Property rights may be incomplete when unforeseen circumstances create opportunities for the buyer and seller to behave in ways unanticipated when the contract was negotiated. Incomplete property rights can provide buyers and sellers with opportunities to behave perfunctorily by exploiting ambiguities and loopholes for their own gain and at the other's greater expense. Sellers may cut costs by using lower-quality inputs or they can reduce their effort – shirk – to save on labor costs. If the buyer has not fully specified the exact attributes of the product they seek, the seller can "gold plate" the product by adding elements that do not meet the buyer's needs but increase the seller's profits. The parties may be reluctant to enter a contract if, due to unclear rules, they are uncertain about the distribution of costs and benefits.

Buyers and sellers frequently find it difficult to fully define property rights in market exchanges. There may be uncertainty about when a product is fully delivered, for example, because the product's true quality characteristics only become apparent through use (e.g., a car). In such circumstances, product quality can only be known after the exchange occurs and the seller uses the product. Contract provisions and public law can sometimes specify whether and how the seller is obligated to provide quality guarantees if the product falls short of the agreed-upon quality. There may also be ambiguity regarding property rights to innovations or other value-creating developments during the contract term. Was it the seller's initiative that led to the improved product, or was it, in fact, the buyer's users who invested time and resources into making the improvements? For example, property rights for a customized IT system or a job training program are often less clearly defined. Such services are inherently more complex than groceries, they are often tailored to the individual user, and there are rarely existing market standards for verifying property rights under different scenarios. Specification of property rights in all scenarios is difficult and likely to leave the buyer and seller uncertain about the true value and costs during the contract exchange.

The problem of incomplete property rights is prominent in government purchasing. Governments often purchase more complex products, such as military equipment or specialized software systems for its unique products and services. More complex products can require more detailed contracts to specify all the quality dimensions, exchange terms, and contingencies. Regulations requiring environmental performance, transparency, or other social provisions make the product yet more complex and further exacerbate the challenge of specifying the buyer and seller rights and obligations. Lack of clearly defined property rights thus represents a fundamental friction in government contracting, creating uncertainty around the allocation of responsibility, risks, and costs.

3.2.5 Independence in Consumption and Production

Under ideal market conditions, all costs and benefits of production and consumption are "internal" to the exchange. Internal means that the seller bears all the costs of production, and the buyer receives all the benefits from the product. Sometimes, however, an exchange yields additional costs and benefits that extend beyond the buyer and seller and are not reflected in the price, commonly referred to as externalities. An externality is a consequence of an activity that is borne by someone who is not party to a market exchange and who did not choose to incur it. Externalities are a market friction; they cause a misalignment of incentives so that exchanges do not result in win–win outcomes, at least for those who would bear the externality's consequences.

With a negative externality, the benefits accrue only to the producer while some of the costs accrue to others. Negative externalities tend to be overproduced – because the distribution of costs and benefits incentivizes the producer to increase production to the detriment of overall social welfare. Pollution is a negative externality because the producer receives the benefits of selling the product while other people endure the pollution's harm to their health. With a positive externality, the producer bears the full cost of production, while some of the benefits accrue to others. While more positive externalities production would benefit society, they tend to be under-produced because the producer receives only a small share of their benefits. If there were no market frictions for the exchange, the externality's producers and recipients could treat the externality as a product to be bought and sold. The recipients could pay the seller to produce more positive externalities and less negative externalities up to the point where the seller's costs would exceed the recipients' total benefits (Alchian and Demsetz 1972). Government policies often look to target problems that arise when the costs of an action are divorced from its benefits. Noise ordinances prevent late night revelry at one house from disturbing the neighborhood's good sleep, and pollution regulations limit harm to ecosystems and human health.

Externalities often permeate government purchasing. Many government purchasing regulations can be understood as efforts to manage externalities. Information disclosure requirements can be seen as externality production requirements. Complying with these requirements can raise costs for the buyer and seller, while the benefits of the disclosed information accrue to overseers and other stakeholders who can be more confident the transaction was not tainted by corruption. Regulations can also address more common externalities, such as environmental protection. Government purchasing regulations that require sellers to achieve environmental performance look to alleviate harms to ecosystems and people that were caused as by-products of production (Behravesh et al. 2022; Darnall, Ji, and Potoski 2017; Dimand et al. 2023a).

3.2.6 Transaction Costs

Most of the attention on the cost of government purchasing focuses on the purchase price – how much money the government paid to the seller. After all, the price is the only cost of the exchange when market conditions are ideal. Of course, real-world purchasing also carries the risk of losses should the purchase end up performing worse than anticipated. The purchase price and risk are not all of the costs of purchasing. Every purchase requires expending resources to find sellers, evaluate their offerings, pay the seller, and take possession of the product. Transaction costs are the resources buyers and sellers expend to make the exchange happen (Williamson 1979, 1981, 1985).

Transaction costs are market frictions because they reduce the value buyers and sellers receive from the exchange. Search and screening costs incur before a purchase, such as specifying the buyer's product needs and identifying sellers and their offerings. Bargaining and transfer costs are incurred as the exchange is negotiated and resources exchanged. Monitoring and enforcement costs are incurred after the exchange and include things such as evaluating product quality and enforcing contract terms. Management activities are costs and resources the government expends for the exchange. Defining needs and evaluating products, writing contract terms, receiving ownership of a product, evaluating quality, all take time, money, and effort. In some cases, transaction costs can be so high as to prevent buyers and sellers from executing what would otherwise have been value-enhancing exchanges (Marvel and Marvel 2007; Bel and Fageda 2009). Table 3 lists types of transaction costs and examples of how market frictions can cause them.

Each of the frictions presented so far ended with an explanation for why the friction was likely to be larger in government purchasing than in private purchasing. Government purchasing is likely to occur with less market competition, more incomplete information, more externalities, and less complete property rights. Each friction creates the need for additional transaction cost expenditures: The buyer and private seller need to spend additional resources to find exchange partners, define requirements and exchange rules, negotiate contract terms, and execute the exchange (Potoski, Petersen, and Brown 2023). These actions are contract management activities that government buyers can implement to mitigate frictions and harness public value. In the next section, we discuss contract management responses to frictions, with a focus on how formal and relational contract management approaches can encourage consummate behavior and minimize perfunctory behavior.

3.3 Market Frictions and Government Contract Management

The framework presented in Section 3.2 identifies challenges that can undermine the value from contracting. Government contracting pursues a broader range of values for the products being purchased, how they are purchased, and how they are delivered. Government contracting, for example, pursues fairness, transparency, and responsiveness to political overseers. Market frictions can undermine all of these values. Insufficient competition may mean there are no

Table 3 Transaction cost categories

Type of Transaction Cost	Time	Source	Management Activity Examples
Search and screening	Prior to exchange	Lack of knowledge about exchange opportunities: stakeholders' demand, supply, and quality of goods	Requirements definition; Evaluating bids
Bargaining and transfer	During exchange	Ambiguity about rights and obligations in the transaction; the cost of exchanging resources	Contract specification; Receiving product
Monitoring and enforcement	After exchange	Difficulty in discerning adherence to terms of the agreement, problems in enforcing terms	Monitoring and evaluation; Renegotiation

Source: Authors' compilation.

suitable products to buy at fair prices. Incomplete information may leave contract managers without an accurate view of the needs and problems the purchase is to address. A seller may look to exploit the loopholes of an incomplete contract, while the buyer's asset-specific investments make it too costly to find an alternative vendor.

Contract management looks to identify the challenges of contracting and deploy activities to mitigate their costs and risks. In many governments around the world, professional contract management staff perform much of the contract management work, from defining needs and requirements to monitoring quality and making payments (Warren 2014). These managers generally work in specialized units tasked with managing contracts on behalf of a broader agency. In one sense, these managers look very much like many other civil service employee. The managers are accountable to executive and legislative overseers through hierarchical channels of authority. Contract management positions require specific qualifications, including training in the unique context and regulatory apparatus of government purchasing, and they are covered under the general umbrella of civil service protections and regulations.

Two key management questions are how to write the contract and how to manage the relationship in the exchange. In the remainder of this section, we discuss how these management activities are responses to market frictions. Our discussion shows that there is no one-size-fits-all approach to managing contracting; different combinations of management activities and approaches can be used to achieve public value in different circumstances.

Perhaps the most important management activity is crafting contract terms – the product, exchange, and governance rules – that structure the buyer and sellers' rights and obligations, which can be more or less complete (Hart and Moore 1988; Hart, Shleifer, and Vishny 1997; Tirole 1999). At first glance, it might seem that writing detailed contract terms are a panacea for every friction that threatens contract value. Specifying product details can improve the prospects that the seller will deliver the sought-after value, including social values such as environmental externalities. A contract might also require sellers to disclose information about production processes or the final product so that the buyer can ensure the requirements have been met. Or a contract might require that the product conform to other uses, thus avoiding asset-specific investments and lock-in problems.

In contrast, if market frictions are relatively small, contracts can be specified to cover just about all potential contingencies, such as when a government buys common office supplies or other off-the-shelf commodities. However, higher levels of market frictions increase the costs of acquiring information, negotiating a contract, and ensuring its terms have been met. A problem may defy description through contract terms and buyers may not know how much value products would offer toward that problem. At some point, the severity of the market frictions raises the transaction costs above the benefits of writing and executing a more detailed contract. The result may be an exchange with the costs and risks of a contract that is yet more incomplete, of the failure to realize value if the exchange is not attempted.

Incomplete contracts raise two important issues for contract design and management. The first issue is whether the buyer or seller will bear the costs and benefits should unanticipated circumstances disrupt the distribution of value in the exchange, what we refer to default risk. The holder of the default risk must accept changes in the value. In a cost-reimbursement contract, for example, the government bears residual risks. The government must pay more if for unforeseen reasons production costs turn out to be higher. The second issue is that incomplete contracts allow buyer and seller discretion. Discretion means that the government or the seller may choose to behave in ways that change the value they and the other party receives, without fear of legal recourse from the other. A buyer or seller may choose perfunctory behavior that yields small gains for the performer but imposes greater losses on the other side (Hart and Moore 2008), all while conforming to the "letter" of the contract as enforceable by a court of law. For example, a seller might reduce their costs by using substandard materials (though still allowed by the contract), even though the materials reduce the quality of the product for the buyer. A buyer may behave perfunctorily by opportunistically exploiting contract terms to raise the seller's production costs above the negotiated price, even though a cheaper production method would meet his needs almost as well.

Buyers and sellers can also use discretion to choose to behave consummately. Consummate behavior decreases the performer's gains while producing greater gains for the other side. For example, the seller might increase their costs by investing a dollar in more research and development, while raising the buyer's value by two dollars through improved product quality. Or a buyer may provide a seller full compensation for delayed delivery that was outside the control of the seller even though the contract allows the buyer to provide reduced compensation.[6]

The potential for perfunctory behavior is caused by a combination of market frictions. Incomplete information and the costs of specifying all the details of the exchange under different contingencies result in incomplete contracts that increase the risk of perfunctory behavior. As a result, a seller may find opportunities to exploit a contract loophole for their own gain and the buyer's greater expense. When facing the potential for perfunctory behavior, contract management may look for remedy by reducing the cause of the frictions, thus allowing the contract to be more complete. Or managers may aim to address the consequences by focusing on mitigating perfunctory behavior.

Governments can address the potential for perfunctory behavior through different combinations of management activities, what we call contract management approaches. The traditional approach to government contract management, often called the formal approach, attempts to target the sources of market frictions (Gutiérrez-Meave et al. 2025). Formal contract management pursues more complete contracts to specify as much as possible about the exchange to

---

[6] We set aside legally enforceable violations of contract terms, such as fraud and theft, except to note that they obviously happen. In these instances, there is little room for contract management except to bring the force of law against the transgressor, or simply exit the exchange and accept the loss.

limit discretion and the risk of perfunctory behavior. Contract managers expend resources to detail product characteristics, delivery terms, and governance rules that structure the relationship and ensure sufficient information to evaluate performance (Dyer and Chu 2003; Petersen et al. 2019). For instance, the contract may specify how often the parties meet and oblige the seller to collect and share data. Consequently, management activities focus on detailing contract terms, acquiring information, and monitoring performance (Anguelov 2020).

Formal contracting uses the contract to structure the relationship between the buyer and the seller. An upside of the formal approach is that the detailed contract offers the buyer and seller more clear incentives and behavior standards for producing value – the buyer and sellers' costs are well defined and justified by the benefits they will receive (Li et al. 2024). Consummate behavior is not an optional choice but is required in the contract. Another upside is that the detailed contract provides less opportunity and incentive for perfunctory behavior; neither side has much opportunity to exploit loopholes at the other's expense. One of formal contracting's downsides is that even the most detailed contract may not specify all the future circumstances of the exchange, leaving the buyer and seller with some measure of discretion to behave perfunctorily (Hart and Moore 2008). Meanwhile, writing, monitoring, and enforcing contract terms bring substantial transaction costs (DeSchepper et al. 2015; Potoski, Petersen, and Brown 2023). Moreover, an excessively prescriptive contract detail may be a disincentive for consummate behavior (Baker, Gibbons, and Murphy 2002). Focusing on rules and compliance can lead to a confrontational and self-interest focused relationship between the buyer and the seller (Baker, Gibbons, and Murphy 2002), while reducing incentives for either party to find ways to benefit the other through consummate behavior.

The relational approach to contract management aims to promote consummate behavior through contract terms that are flexible and purposively grant the seller autonomy (Poppo and Zenger 2002; Lamothe and Lamothe 2012). A goal is to use flexible contract terms to harness the seller's expertise and produce more value (Amirkhanyan, Kim, and Lambright 2012). This approach requires building and managing relations based on trust, mutual understanding, and reciprocity (Frydlinger et al. 2021; Gutiérrez-Meave et al. 2025), in which each side accepts the potential for small losses in return for greater gains from their partner's cooperation. Relational contracting aims to incentivize cooperation by creating conditions in which both parties value the future, each party may reciprocate behavior in response to their partner's behavior, and the buyer and seller engage in multiple sequential opportunities to choose between consummate and perfunctory behavior (Axelrod and Hamilton 1981). When the partners are better informed, they can better interpret the other's behavior and can better identify opportunities to produce more value for the relationship, leading to a more accurate discernment of whether the behavior was intended to be consummate or perfunctory. Parties are more likely to value the future when there are potential gains from future exchanges or when reputations are at stake (Tadelis 1999). A seller that has a reputation for consummate behavior is a more attractive partner for exchanges with others in the future. Repeated interactions incentivize cooperation because consummate behavior in one decision may be reciprocated by subsequent consummate behavior, leading to a virtuous cooperative cycle (Frydlinger, Hart, and Vitasek 2019; Li et al. 2024).

Contract managers can look to shape the exchange toward a more formal or relational approach, such as by reducing discretion, creating more opportunities for repeated interactions, and incentivizing consummate behavior (Frydlinger, Hart, and Vitasek 2019; Frydlinger et al. 2021). Purchasing tends toward more formal approaches when products are simpler and frictions are smaller. When a government purchases a commodity, such as a desk or printer paper, the contract and public law tend to be more complete, and there is less room for the parties to choose consummate or perfunctory behavior. In contrast, when a product is more complex and frictions are larger, the buyer and seller have more room for discretion (Brown, Potoski, and Van Slyke 2016; Domingos et al. 2025).

Discretion of course does not guarantee that the buyer and seller end up in the virtuous cycle of consummate cooperation that relational contracting pursues. Consummate cooperation is more likely when the buyer and seller have multiple opportunities to engage in sequential behavior, with each able to observe and respond to their partner's previous cooperation. The circumstances for sustaining relational contracting may be hard to obtain; government buyers and sellers may be guided by different values (Piatak and Jensen 2024), the parties may be unable to perceive each other's actions as cooperative, or regulations may prevent buyers from considering sellers' reputations when making purchases. Even under ideal circumstances, the virtuous cycle of cooperation can be difficult to initiate if the exchange creates few and nonsequential choices between consummate and perfunctory behavior, and longer-term reputations may be insufficient incentive for consummate choices. Even after initial consummate interactions, discretion may result in perfunctory behavior because of ambiguities and lack of mutual understanding. The end may be a negative spiral where one party's perfunctory behavior induces cascading retaliatory responses of perfunctory behavior (Hart and Moore 2008, p. 8).

While contract design and management practices can push an exchange toward a more formal or relational direction, every exchange ends up incorporating some degree of both formal and relational elements (Poppo and Zenger 2002; Lamothe and Lamothe 2012). Even the most detailed contract still leaves some room for discretion in which the buyer and seller may choose to pursue a cooperative relationship based on consummate behavior. Likewise, even if the buyer and seller aim for cooperation and relational contracting, their interactions remain bound by public law and contract regulations that limit the extent to which government contract managers can exercise discretion, for example in choosing which sellers to award the contract to or in how to interpret the written terms of the contract.

Our discussion in this section suggests important insights for analyses of contracting and contract management. Market frictions shed light on the challenges of contracting in different circumstances and suggest potential management activities to address them. The same frictions may be addressed by different contract management approaches – formal and relational contracting each comes with trade-offs. When frictions are high, formal contracting requires more transaction cost expenditures to mitigate the frictions and address their consequences. Relational contracting avoids much of these costs by relying on less precise contract terms and the expectation of more consummate behavior through a relationship of trust and reciprocity. However, the downside is greater losses should that relationship fail to materialize. Our framework also suggests that just about every contract has both formal and relational elements. A relational exchange occurring among close and cooperative partners is still grounded in a legal structure that provides formal provisions against fraud and theft. Formal contracts inevitably leave room for discretion and the potential for both cooperative relationships that promote mutual gain and conflictual relationships that lead to lost value.

3.4 Section Summary

In this section, we have introduced market frictions – lack of competition, information problems, non-fungible assets, externalities, incomplete property rights, and transaction costs – as a conceptual lens for diagnosing government contracting challenges. We have also discussed market frictions as the sources of the challenges that contract management needs to address to harness public value. Rather than assigning contract problems to the absence of contract management activities (e.g., the government did not write the contract with sufficient detail or did not perform sufficient contract monitoring), our framework directs analytical attention to the root causes of contracting challenges. The term "friction" suggests that these challenges are a matter of degree and that few if any government purchases take place without the presence of one or more frictions. For each friction, we discussed circumstances in government contracting where these frictions are often larger and more common. Contract scholars and practitioners can use this framework to diagnose contract problems and identify management activities that can effectively address them.

Our framework suggests that market conditions are not simply influenced by buyers and sellers but can also be influenced by activities people perform. Contract management seeks to choose the mix of activities to yield the best outcome for government purchases. Merely following the traditional playbook of sequentially executing contract management activities may not deliver value; governments may pursue activities unsuited to the specific frictions in the purchase. We outlined two common approaches – formal and relational contracting – that contract managers can use to address frictions. Formal contracting seeks to direct buyers and sellers to consummate behavior by writing product, exchange, and governance rules based on the assumption that sellers have incentives toward perfunctory behavior in areas where the contract is incomplete or weakly enforced. Relational contracting, by contrast, grants buyers and sellers more discretion based on the assumption that the parties are more likely to behave consummately for shared value. We return to these two contract management approaches in Section 5.

For contracting to work well, contract managers must be able to diagnose market frictions in a purchase, understand how these frictions increase costs and threaten public value, and identify activities that can mitigate it, ultimately improving contract outcomes. These are not simple tasks. Government purchases are often characterized by multiple frictions, making the contracting problem hard to diagnose. In addition, frictions can influence each other – for example, asymmetric information can increase the buyer's transaction costs for doing market and product search, but the buyer's investment of resources in search activities is also likely to reduce the information asymmetry. Diagnosis and treatment of market frictions require a range of skills and knowledge in the government purchasing workforce. A lack of appropriate skills in diagnosing and treating market frictions can result in a loss of public value, with purchases leaving the government worse off than expected, as illustrated by the examples of failed purchases in Section 1. The next step in our framework is to present a human resource perspective that focuses on skills for diagnosing and treating market frictions in contracting.

4 Contract Management Skills for Market Frictions

We have so far shown how market frictions offer an analytical lens for diagnosing government contracting challenges and identifying contract management responses. Market frictions can undermine the value proposition of government contracting if contract management does not adequately diagnose and treat the purchase's frictions. We also presented two common approaches for addressing market frictions: formal and relational contract management. The success of government contract management in diagnosing and treating market frictions depends, at least in part, on the skills and knowledge of the contracting workforce that oversees and implements management activities. Misdiagnosing the governments' need and poorly executing management activities in response to frictions puts the value of a purchase at risk. If market frictions set the conditions and challenges under which government purchasing takes place, analyzing the value of a market exchange requires understanding the skills of the contract managers who execute the exchange.

In this section, we introduce the third concept in our framework: the skills of government contract managers. We thereby introduce a human resource dimension that is rarely present in the economic and public management contracting literature (for a few exceptions, see Snider and Rendon 2012; Dimand et al. 2023a). Unlike the extensive lists of contract management skills available in the private purchasing literature (Giunipero and Pearcy 2000; Kartunen 2018; Bals et al. 2019; Schulze, Bals, and Johnsen 2019), our framework starts from market frictions as the underlying root causes of contract challenges that skills must address. We show how our framework can be applied to identify the skills for effective contract management. We begin Section 4.1 by introducing the human resource perspective and defining skills. Then, in Section 4.2, we apply our framework to identify a range of skills that can diagnose and mitigate frictions in ways that harness public value. Finally, in Section 4.3, we provide a summary of the section and discuss how market frictions and contract skills frequently occur in combinations in real-world purchasing scenarios.

4.1 Human Resources and Government Contract Management

Effective contract management requires skills and knowledge to diagnose and treat the causes and consequences of market frictions. A public purchaser needs skills to specify product requirements, possess clear knowledge of relevant procurement rules and regulation, communicate effectively with sellers, and accurately monitor product or service quality, just to mention a few. More importantly, these skills need to be applied in ways that effectively diagnose and mitigate market frictions. To identify skills for government contracting, we draw on the human resource literature for conceptual foundations, where human capital has long been associated with organizational performance (Wright, Dunford, and Snell 2001; Deist and Winterton 2005). We also draw on public management research identifying public sector contracting skills and activities (Warren 2014; Girth et al. 2012), along with concepts developed in the private sector purchasing literature (Tassabehji and Moorhouse 2008; Derwik and Hellström 2017; Stek and Schiele 2021). Finally, we draw on human resource classifications that focus on procurement activities (McCue, Prier, and Steinfeld 2018) and public contracting topical subjects that appear in course materials (Snider and Rendon 2012).

Our framework begins with market frictions and management activities and then identifies the skills that can diagnose and address frictions in ways that harness value. This approach aligns with how the human resource management field often conceptualizes skills: The value of a skill lies in applying it in ways that obtain intended goals (Wright, Dunford, and Snell 2001; Getha-Taylor 2008). In government contracting, this entails diagnosing the market friction(s) that shape contracting challenges and performing activities that treat market frictions. Importantly, this does not entail making the friction go away – purchases involving high asset-specific investments are likely to be exchanged in incomplete markets (Girth et al. 2012) – but treating the friction in a way that harnesses public value. Different skills can have different or similar cost–benefit calculus. For instance, skill A may produce more value than doing nothing, skill B produces more value than A, and skill C produces the same value as B.

We differentiate between knowledge and skills (e.g., McClelland 1973; Cheetham and Chivers 1996). We use "skill" to refer to the procedures and tasks that a person must be able to do to perform in their job or work function (Cheetham and Chivers 1996; Turco and Maggioni 2022). "Skill" in this sense is distinct from "knowledge." We use the term "knowledge" to refer to acquired information – either through direct observation or the provision of information – about a subject area, task, or activity.[7] For example, a person can acquire knowledge about typing – where to place hands and which fingers move to different keys – by watching others do it. The skill of typing, though, comes from applying this knowledge through practice to learn the ability to type quickly and accurately. To be clear, undertaking a specific contract activity does not equate to a "skill" in our framework. Instead, we use "skill" in a more specific and precise way – the utilization of a contract management activity to either diagnose or treat a market friction. For example, writing a highly detailed contract is not, in and of itself, an example of a "skill" in our framework. "Skill" is determining whether expending resources to write a detailed contract effectively addresses the underlying friction and then drafting the contract to mitigate its root cause.

---

[7] A related term to "skill" is "competency," the ability to properly implement a cluster of skills in a workplace environment or as part of a workplace task or function (Gubbins and Dooley 2021).

To diagnose and treat market frictions, contract managers require a range of different types of skills and knowledge. Before proceeding, it is important to emphasize the complex interdependencies between market frictions and contracting skills. A first complexity is that the frictions and skills we identify contain some overlap. For example, noncompetitive markets can lead to market frictions, while non-fungible assets can be a cause of noncompetitive markets. A second complexity is that the magnitude of market frictions also depends, at least partially, on the buyer and seller's execution of contract management activities. For example, writing better contract terms can improve the allocation of property rights, but contract writing is also itself a source of transaction costs expenditures. Market frictions and contract management activities are therefore endogenous; market frictions and skills are endogenous; and contract management and skills are endogenous. Frictions, activities, and skills appear in numbers, combinations, and causal relationships exceeding what we can reasonably cover here. Our presentation of how different contract management activities can be deployed to diagnose and treat market frictions therefore aims to be illustrative rather than comprehensive – instead of providing an exhaustive list, we show how an analysis of market frictions helps identify relevant contract management skills that can harness public value in government contracting.

4.2 Skills for Managing Market Frictions

In this section, we examine each of the six market frictions presented in Section 3, focusing on how public contract management skills can help diagnose and treat each friction. We do this aware, as noted Sections 3 and 4.1, that the market frictions and skills may appear in realistic government purchasing scenarios in combinations too numerous to cover here. Our aim is to demonstrate how analyzing market frictions and management activities can lead to insights about skills – a framework that can inform contract management analysis beyond the specific examples covered in this section.

Table 4 identifies the market frictions and accompanying illustrative diagnostic and treatment skills, which we elaborate on in the subsequent sections. Some of the skills in our framework are specific to the contract management profession, such as market diagnosis and market management, requirements definition, and contract design. Other skills are more generic to the public management discipline, such as analytical skills, communication, and cost–benefit analysis. A government contract manager is likely to need both specific and generic skills to effectively diagnose and treat market frictions and their multitude of combinations in real-world contracting scenarios. Consequently,

Table 4 Market frictions and illustrative diagnostic and treatment skills

Market Friction	Diagnostic Skills	Treatment Skills
Incomplete markets	Product diagnosis Market diagnosis	Contract design Market management
Non-fungible assets	Product diagnosis Analytic skills	Contract design
Imperfect information	Requirements definition Capabilities assessment	Information acquisition Communication skills Analytical skills
Incomplete property rights	Contract analysis Business analysis	Contract design
Interdependence in consumption and production of goods	Regulatory analysis Stakeholder mapping	Requirements definition Cost–Benefit analysis
Transaction costs	Cost estimation	Process improvement Strategic thinking

Source: Authors' compilation.

we address both specific and generic skills as part of applying our framework to identify the skills essential for government contract management.

4.2.1 Incomplete Markets and Skills

As discussed in Section 3.2.1, governments often buy the same products as many firms and citizens, such as automobiles, office supplies, and even cafeteria food. Governments, however, also purchase a range of products and services where competition is low or absent, which increases the risk of higher prices and lower quality. Facing markets with weak competition, government contract managers can draw on several skills for diagnosing and treating the resulting frictions. Identifying market competition may seem as simple as counting the number of sellers, an approach to contracting popularized by Steve Goldsmith, Mayor of Indianapolis, Indiana, in the 1980s (Goldsmith 1997). Back then, the World Wide Web did not yet exist, and consumers would consult a large physical book, colloquially known as the "The Yellow Pages," to find sellers. The Yellow Pages listed product categories (barber shops, plumbing services, dentists, etc.) along with businesses offering to sell the products. Mayor Goldsmith argued that if the Yellow Pages listed a handful of businesses for a product, the market was sufficiently competitive for the government to buy the product rather than make it. Diagnosing market competition through devices such as the Yellow Pages tests is alluring – they are simple to implement and require few skills. Their limitation, however, is that like a thermometer for measuring fever, they report only the severity of the symptom and not its cause. More complete diagnoses identify both a symptom and its underlying cause(s).

Public contract managers skilled in diagnosing the degree of market competition can accurately assess whether they are purchasing from a market where (at least) several sellers compete on relatively equal terms or if one or a few enjoy a competitive advantage. Two contract management skills can be used to help identify the causes of market competition: market diagnosis and product diagnosis. *Market diagnosis* is the ability to analyze market attributes that create barriers to competition, such as circumstances where one company has exclusive access to strategic resources that lower its production costs and understand how and where these barriers create opportunities for perfunctory behavior by the seller. Government policy can also influence market competition. Purchasing regulations (e.g., license requirements for sellers) can create entry barriers as potential competitors face high costs to navigate the regulatory thicket that incumbents have already mastered. Barriers to competition can occur simultaneously: A company with strategic resource advantages might petition the government to require other firms to overcome newly installed regulatory hurdles. *Product diagnosis* is the ability to understand how a product's production processes, inputs, and costs can create barriers for entry by other firms. For example, the diagnosis can assess whether production requires high fixed costs or scarce and valuable resources and inputs. Such analyses can help managers identify products that are prone to noncompetitive markets such as gas or electricity production and distribution due to natural monopoly, network effects, high start-up costs, or scarce inputs that advantage the incumbent seller (Joaquin and Greitens 2012).

Identifying the cause of weak competition opens the path to treatment. When a government receives only a single bid or the "Yellow Pages" test suggests only a single (or few) potential seller(s), the appropriate treatment depends on why there was so little competition. Other potential sellers may have been unaware of the opportunity; they may have assumed that the incumbent seller would have a competitive advantage in the bidding process; or they may have anticipated high start-up costs from learning to navigate public procurement regulations. For contract managers, an important skill is the ability to match the treatment to the underlying cause. If the underlying cause is a product characteristic (e.g., natural monopoly), the treatment should focus on the attributes of the product. Alternatively, if the primary driver of limited competition is a market characteristic (e.g., licensure requirements to sell a product), then treatment should focus on overcoming or eliminating the market barrier to competition.

Market management is the ability to mitigate or eliminate barriers to entry and facilitate the entry of new sellers (Brown and Potoski 2006; Girth et al.

2012). A lack of competition can stem from the characteristics of the market and product, or government policies and regulation. Companies are likely to build their competitive strategies around these underlying drivers. Market management skills can help address conditions of limited competition (Johnston and Girth 2012; Brogaard, Petersen, and Madsen 2025). For example, if limited competition stems from a scarce resource, such as a particular skill in the supplier workforce, the contract manager can look for ways to make the resource more widely available, such as by offering training to multiple firms. Or a manager may design a contract that requires the dominant firm to subcontract with more suppliers. This practice can stimulate competition over inputs in the short term, and potentially develop viable competitors for the entire product in the long term. Alternatively, if the barrier to entry is government-induced, the market management treatment may be the ability to engage bureaucratic and policy processes to mitigate or eliminate the entry barriers. For example, a contract manager might request a short-term exemption from a licensure requirement and participate in the policymaking process to remove the licensure requirement in the long term.

When low competition is the result of product characteristics, a path to treatment can be found in how the purchase is structured. *Contract design* includes the ability to design contract terms to promote competition (Girth et al. 2012). When confronting a natural monopoly, a traditional response has been to accept its existence and issue regulations to limit the seller's ability to raise prices and lower quality. Here the skill is the ability to craft a contract with incentives that balances a reasonable return for the seller with the costs incurred by the jurisdiction's consumers (Hartmann et al. 2014). Better understanding the cause of weak competition can suggest alternative and complementary treatments. When the lack of competition is due to high fixed costs and low marginal costs, it may be possible to decompose the product into high fixed cost and low marginal cost components. The high fixed cost components may remain a natural monopoly, while the low marginal cost components may be amenable to competitive markets. For example, electrical utility companies have traditionally been treated as natural monopolies because of the high fixed costs for building the power plant and distribution lines. New technologies such as small-scale solar generation can now produce electricity with relatively low fixed costs. Electricity production can thus have more competitive markets, while distribution remains a natural monopoly.

When products can be decomposed into high and low marginal cost components, skilled contract design can provide stronger incentives for sellers to deliver value. A cost-reimbursement contract provides the seller with a fixed return in exchange for his efforts and inputs. Sellers may favor cost reimbursement contracts for high fixed costs. Sellers may underprice the initial units to win the contract in anticipation of having a cost advantage in later sales when competing with sellers who have not made the fixed cost investments. Contract design skill helps better structure different purchases. By recognizing the fixed and variable cost structures, public contract managers can design the contract so that the number of units sold covers all the units the government needs to purchase, allowing vendors to compete on equal grounds.

4.2.2 Non-Fungible Assets and Skills

Non-fungible assets are resources that lose value when put to an alternative use outside the contract due to specialized investments. For the government buyer, the market friction arises because, having invested in the specific asset, the seller is able to raise prices or lower quality (Levin and Tadelis 2010). Asset specificity can be a challenging construct to diagnose. The challenge originates from the fact that investments become specific through how products are produced and used, rather than characteristics of the market. Products requiring specialized investments may initially have competitive markets; the vendor making the specialized investments for the first sale may then be at a disadvantage in subsequent negotiations. The seller may lose value if subsequent sales do not occur, giving buyers an opportunity to drive down prices. Specialized investments by the buyer can likewise create problems – sellers can take advantage if the buyer loses value by not purchasing more of the seller's products.

Identifying asset-specific investments require *product diagnosis skills,* which includes the ability to understand the essential requirements of the production process, the types of investments the seller has to make to produce the product, and the investments the purchasing government has to make to use the product. *Analytic skills* to support this include the ability to answer questions such as: Once a vendor creates a production process for this product, could they easily transform the process to make a similar product for a different client? Could the government easily adopt a product from another seller, without making additional investments? If the answer to these questions is "no," then the government is likely purchasing a product requiring specialized investments. If the answer is "yes," the next level of product diagnosis skill is the ability to identify the source of the specific investment and how the investments become manifest in the product. Here knowledge of the product's components becomes essential (Fernandez 2007) – government purchasers need to know which components are fungible and which are asset-specific.

While they may have different causes, specialized investments and natural monopolies manifest similar symptoms. In both cases, there can be limited competition in subsequent offerings for the product. The *contract design* skills for treating natural monopoly can be applied to products requiring specialized investments. Contract design skills can help decompose the product into components that require specialized investments and those that are more fungible. This can have the dual benefit of immediate competition in the initial offering and subsequent competition in next round offerings for the fungible components, while also providing other firms' opportunities to learn what is required to offer the specialized component. Participating in the production and assembly of a specialized product can provide firms with information at a much lower cost than if they were on the outside of the exchange looking in.

Public contract managers can likewise sometimes design contracts that break the specialized components of a product into a research and development component and a separate build-and-deliver component. Contract managers can employ a firm to design and develop the system and insist that the underlying codes are delivered open source as part of the purchase once they are finalized. Contract managers can also create down-select processes, where prospective firms compete to offer solutions for the specialized investment components and the chosen firm is required to use the other competent firms as subcontractors. Here again, the contract manager is hedging on the risk of becoming locked into a single vendor for the specific component of an exchange. Alternatively, the contract manager can require the vendor to work closely with government employees in the design and development of the specific component or in the implementation phase to ensure that knowledge transfer passes from the seller to the government. Such requirements for passing on the design specifications can be written into the contract.

4.2.3 Incomplete Information and Skills

Government purchasing often occurs under conditions where information is incomplete. Buyers and sellers do not have full information about markets, products, and all other buyers and sellers, which can affect the price and quality of the products that governments buy (Akerlof 1970). When governments buy products with monopoly attributes or that require asset-specific investments, there are often few sellers; as a result, there is scant information in the market about the range of products, their attributes, and prices. When a government purchaser seeks to buy a "solution," they may struggle to identify the types of products and services that might resolve or ameliorate the problem. There may be multiple sellers offering different products across a range of prices, but it may be difficult to discern ex ante trade-offs among products' performance and prices, and even whether a vendor is offering a "lemon." Similarly, governments may buy products whose quality is more difficult to measure (e.g., wrap-around medical services or information technology systems). When governments enter the market for these types of products, there may be many options available, but little information about how well they will perform in addressing the government's needs.

A buyer can diagnose her level of information through her ability to precisely define the product she seeks to purchase or the problem she wants the purchase to solve. The skill of *requirements definition* is the ability to specify precise product qualities and exchange terms (Hartmann et al. 2014). When information is relatively complete, the buyer can more easily express in writing the precise specifications of the product or the specific steps the seller should take to produce and deliver the product. If the buyer is unable to define requirements, a likely culprit is incomplete information. If the buyer is unable to define requirements, she may instead assess the seller's capabilities to produce the value she seeks. The skill of *capabilities assessment* is the ability to determine if a seller can make a product to meet the buyer's needs, even if the ideal product has yet to be produced. Capabilities assessment involves acquiring information about a seller's capacity and competencies (Romzek and Johnston 2002), say for innovation or research and development, rather than an assessment of a specific existing product. Capabilities assessment can be based on the seller's past performance on related challenges or for other customers.

When incomplete information impairs purchasing, treatments include acquiring more information and making better use of the information that is available. The skill of *information acquisition* is the ability to acquire information and organizing it to provide insights for decision-making. Information can come from multiple sources and can include insights on several features of the exchange (Chen and Perry 2003; Fernandez 2007; Michelsen and de Boer 2009), including the following:

- The types of products and how they meet purchasing needs
- Differentiating product attributes (e.g., qualities of the product; prices of different product offerings)
- The needs of the ultimate user in the government organization
- The capabilities of sellers that might offer the product
- Features of the product or the exchange that create opportunities for perfunctory behavior by the seller.

For the first two types of information – products and product attributes – the focus is on acquiring "hard data" about tangible features of the product. Does the police car have the requisite engine and safety features? Will cleaning services empty waste bins? Information sources might include direct observation, reading descriptions of the product, prepurchase testing of the product, or reports from past or current customers.

For the remaining three types of information – user needs, seller capabilities, and opportunities for perfunctory behavior – there may still be a need for such hard data. Buyers can solicit verifiable input from service recipients, other government employees, legislators and political overseers, and technical and scientific experts. Often, however, needs, capabilities, and opportunities to behave in a manner that deviates from the win–win spirit of the contract may also be "softer" qualities that are difficult to assess through direct observation, often because the information has social elements that defy direct observation or summation in written communication. Users' satisfaction with a product, for example, may depend greatly on seemingly small or difficult to describe differences in product features and quality. Familiarity and expertise with a topic and stakeholder groups can help a government contract manager understand this nuance and detail (McKevitt et al. 2012).

Acquiring information about softer and perhaps more complex qualities such as social elements often requires a back-and-forth exchange between the buyer and the seller. *Communication skills* are the ability to convey and receive complex information in a manner appropriate for the recipient and context. Communication skills help public contract managers enquire and disseminate information about the product they are seeking in terms the seller best understands to gain as much relevant information as possible. Contract managers must be able to engage in an information exchange with different target groups and under very different contexts (Lamothe and Lamothe 2012; Carnochan et al. 2019). Some information comes from the physical world, including the material conditions that influence the ability of a purchasing government to achieve its mission. For example, government organizations that operate in maritime environments (e.g., environmental protection organizations, navies, and coast guards) need products such as boats and ships that can withstand the impact of waves and the corrosive effects of salt water. Other information comes from the social world, including sellers and producers, service recipients, other government employees, legislators and political executives, and technical and scientific experts, with each community having its own expertise, language and communication approaches. Service recipients can have information about how different types of services improve outcomes. Legislators and elected executives may have clearer views of the nature of public opinion on the problem and the public's willingness to spend resources to improve it.

Communication skills can also help the government buyer describe what consummate and perfunctory behaviors look like, and, similarly, what perfunctory behavior looks like. For example, a buyer could use communication skills to convince the seller that when production challenges emerge, joint problem solving is preferred to unilateral decision-making. The buyer may communicate this in a way that convinces the seller that the buyer will approach challenges in the same manner, thereby building trust that the parties will reciprocate consummate behavior. Providing clarity about what types of behavior are desired is critical when there is information asymmetry about a product's qualities and attributes and there are multiple opportunities for the seller, buyer, or both to behave perfunctory.

Government buyers can also treat incomplete information by increasing the value of the information they obtain. Just knowing a fact does not mean the manager can use it well when making a decision. Information requires interpretation and evaluation to have meaning and allow for better decisions. **Analytic skills** are the ability to make sense of information to inform decisions. Analytic skills facilitate translating large amounts of complex and diffuse information into actionable insights that can improve decision-making. The core of analytic skills are mental frameworks that provide structure to information by indicating which information is relevant, how the information can be organized, and how it can be interpreted to provide guidance for decisions (Weick 1979).[8] A framework helps with identifying what conditions are unwanted, whether the conditions are amendable to improvement, and the cause effect and trade-off relations among solutions. Thus, analytic skills help contract managers identify if the segment's literacy is sufficient for the employment opportunities and whether the education program can sufficiently improve it. For contract management, analytical skills can include weighing trade-offs between different offerings to determine what to purchase and evaluating how well a potential product meets the buyer's needs.

4.2.4 Incomplete Property Rights and Skills

We saw in Section 3 that when property rights are incomplete, the buyer and seller's rights and obligations are not sufficiently specified, resulting in ambiguities and loopholes that each party may exploit at the other's expense. Clear and specific property rights can be particularly difficult to achieve in government contracting. One reason for this is that governments often purchase complex products. These products tend to have more important quality dimensions that are difficult to precisely define in a contract and are difficult to measure before and even after the exchange (Brown, Potoski and Van Slyke 2016).

---

[8] Analytic skills in this sense are similar to sensemaking skills proposed by Weick (1979). Sensemaking is the process of understanding and creating meaning from information, thereby improving decision-making (Weick 1979).

The challenge of writing a complete contract can be exacerbated by the process and social values that governments pursue when purchasing. Fairness, transparency, and equal treatment can be difficult qualities for governments to specify in a contract and then monitor and evaluate as the product is delivered. Many laws and regulations intended to promote these values, such as requirements to publicly announce calls for bids, predefined contract award criteria, and contract negotiation procedures, apply only to government purchasing (Warren 2014; McCue, Prier, and Steinfeld 2018). Other public procurement rules require that all suppliers be able to bid on equal terms. These requirements may limit the government buyer's ability to purchase what it needs. A well-known example is the inclusion of rules that prevent a government from specifying that it intends to purchase Apple laptops. Such rules require instead that the government specify performance requirements for the laptops it intends to purchase. A government that wants to purchase an Apple laptop may end up with a Dell or Lenovo laptop. In contrast, a business or private consumer who wants an Apple laptop can simply purchase one. Such rules and regulations can make government purchasing more complex and costly (Tadelis 2012; Potoski, Petersen, and Brown 2023), thus exacerbating the challenges of fully and clearly defining property rights.

Diagnosing imperfections or misalignment in the allocation of property rights requires contract and business analysis skills. The public contract manager can apply these skills to map the allocation of property rights in the exchange and provide insight about where, when, and how the seller might behave perfunctorily to harm the buyer. This allows the buyer to prioritize or triage the treatment steps to reduce the likelihood of a negative outcome. The skill of *contract analysis* is the ability to identify how the allocation of property rights in the contract shape incentives and allow the seller to exercise discretion in an exchange. When property rights are fully delineated and other frictions are trivially small, discretion is narrow and the contract incentives direct seller toward producing value for the buyer. When property rights are incomplete, the seller has discretion for consummate or perfunctory behavior.

As we noted in Section 3, contracts generally include three categories of property rights terms, or rules, designed to ensure that the exchange delivers value to the buyer and the seller. Product rules define the characteristics and capabilities of the product; exchange rules define how the exchange will occur; and governance rules define areas where the buyer, the seller, or both have authority to make decisions. The combination of these rules determines the areas where the seller has discretion. For example, if product and exchange rules are highly specified, there is little discretion for the seller to deviate from contract terms. It is more clear what product qualities the seller must provide and how much they will be paid as a result. If, however, product and exchange terms are unspecified and governance rules are vague, the seller has more discretion to make decisions about the product's inputs and costs (e.g., use cheaper materials, while raising the price) (Hart, Shleifer, and Vishny 1997).

Knowing when a seller has discretion does not indicate what behavior the seller will choose. The skill of *business analysis* is the ability to understand a seller's motivation to predict how the seller will behave when a contract grants discretion. Business analysis is based on understanding the preferences and goals of other businesses, how they view their alternatives, and how they will make decisions. The analysis starts with an ability to understand the seller's preferences – what types of value does the seller receive from the exchange. A simple answer is that sellers want profits and getting the highest price at the lowest cost is the path to doing so. Reality is not so simple – companies use different strategies and business models to achieve profits. For example, a company's strategy may be to pursue profits through lowering costs, with a business model focused on finding efficiencies, perhaps even at the expense of product quality. Other companies pursue profits through a business model based on higher prices for higher quality, perhaps to suit the tastes of narrower market segments.

Business analysis also includes the ability to understand how the contract and context of the exchange shapes opportunities and constraints facing the seller (Hartmann et al. 2014). For example, incomplete information raises strategic choices for sellers as well as buyers; in a lemons market, a seller that would benefit more from selling higher-quality products has incentives to credibly reassure buyers that its products actually have higher qualities that merit higher prices. Finally, the skill includes the ability to analyze information to project how sellers will make decisions under different circumstances. Here the buyer's diagnosis involves anticipating how the seller will behave under the contract's terms and determining what parts of the exchange are most likely to lead to negative outcomes for the buyer. For example, if the contract's exchange terms reimburse the seller for the costs incurred, the seller has the incentive to spend excessively and pass those costs on to the buyer.

Once diagnosed, the treatment for imperfectly assigned property rights can begin with a focus on mitigating the problem's source. Government contract managers can once again draw on the skill of *contract design* to treat the problem. In this context, contract design includes the ability to assign property rights to align the incentives of the buyer and the seller. The three contract rules – product, exchange, and governance – are the building blocks of effective contract design. Crafting complete contract rules draws on the previous skill of requirements definition; here the goal is to specify as clearly as possible the product's attributes and capabilities (Amirkhanyan, Kim, and Lambright 2010; Amirkhanyan 2011).

If product rules are sufficiently defined, the seller does not have discretion to deliver a product that differs from what the buyer wants. However, as noted Section 3.3, in many cases of government purchasing, the buyer knows the problem that they want solved, but not the product that can solve the problem. Sometimes product rules will be left incomplete. Contract managers then may focus on exchange and governance rules to improve contract outcomes (Frydlinger et al. 2021). Designing effective exchange rules draws on social skills that help buyers anticipate how the contract's rules and incentives will influence sellers' behavior and how their choices will change in response to different rules and incentives.

An important piece of contract design is the allocation of risk. Contracts contain risk because there are potential outcomes from the exchange that were not fully anticipated when the buyer and seller agreed to terms. Production costs may be higher, for example, due to unforeseen events like bad weather. Product quality may be higher, perhaps because some feature turns out to be particularly valuable. Here the exercise of effective contract design skills uses exchange and governance rules to assign risk to the party that bears responsibility for making decisions. If the seller has responsibility for making decisions about costs, then exchange rules should be included so that the seller incurs the cost risks (e.g., a fixed price exchange rule) (Lo, Zanarone, and Ghosh 2022). Sellers are incentivized to save on costs and avoid cost overruns if they bear cost risks (and assuming other contract terms prevent reducing product quality). Contract design can promote collaborative decision-making: Governance rules can be incorporated into the contract to require joint decision-making in the contract's gray areas, along with cooperative processes for allocating the costs, benefits, and risks, of those decisions.

4.2.5 Externalities and Skills

Externalities occur when an exchange produces additional costs and benefits not reflected in the price, and which are borne by a party external to the exchange. Externalities are important but complex for government purchasing because government buyers pursue a wide range of product, process, and social values, as we discussed in Section 2. To diagnose the externalities that a government purchase risks producing, contract managers use a comprehensive set of rules and regulations that govern government purchasing (McCue, Prier, and Steinfeld 2018). *Regulatory analysis* is the ability to identify legally required actions for specific circumstances. For government purchasing, this includes the ability to identify legal and regulatory requirements for the generation of externalities in pursuit of social value. For example, procurement regulations specify the type of exchange rule to be used for a class of products (e.g., fixed price contracts for commodities); such a rule is designed to promote the acquisition of products that meet some acceptable quality standard at the lowest possible cost to the government purchaser. Other procurement regulations might require contract managers to direct a portion of their procurement to firms owned and operated by disadvantaged groups (e.g., female or minority-owned firms).

Regulatory analysis can be important because laws and rules that aim to promote externalities may contain overlapping and even contradicting mandates when applied to a specific purchase. In such circumstances, regulatory analysis may therefore need to include an investigation of political processes and preferences to shed light on how to achieve the mandate's intent. Procurement rules and regulations are often designed to provide a benefit to a broader social group (e.g., racial minorities), though there may also be instances where rules aim to prevent a negative externality for a specified group. For example, prohibitions on contracting with firms that rely on child labor dampens negative externalities for minors. Managing externalities through contracting also requires identifying how stakeholders receive the different costs and benefits that spillover through the exchange. The skill of *stakeholder mapping* is the ability to identify the relevant groups impacted by a regulation and how a specific regulation affects their preferences.

Once a public contract manager identifies the targeted externality, the treatment calls for *requirements definition* skills, which can be employed, once again, to translate the societal benefit or public value into a specific requirement of the contract (Brunjes and Rodriquez-Pleza 2024). In this way, the externality becomes either a feature of the product to be purchased or a separate add-on that comes with the product. In the first instance, the contract manager specifies the product features that satisfy the direct user's needs, as well as the product features that generate the positive externality or prevent the negative externality (e.g., environmental requirements). In the second instance, the contract manager may write what amounts to a separate contract to impact the production of the externality as they purchase a product to meet their needs. For example, the contract manager may write a request for proposal which welcomes bids from any supplier for a particular product, and then write an accompanying request for proposal for the very same product but limits bids to minority or female-owned firms.

Because contracting rules and regulations may be overlapping and contradicting, contract managers need to balance competing values. The skill of *cost–benefit analysis* is the ability to identify and prioritize the different values across different products and contract outcomes, and then make purchases that optimize across value dimensions. For example, a contract manager may seek to maximize quality versus price in the open competition purchase, while maximizing equity over quality and price by favoring small businesses or businesses owned by disadvantages groups through a set-aside contract (Brunjes and Rodriquez-Pleza 2024). Assuming that the two purchases are for the same product, this portfolio approach optimizes the trade-offs across a bundle of purchases. The skill of cost–benefit analysis is particularly important for government contracting because of the broader and more complex array of costs and benefits involved when governments purchase.

Requirements definition and cost–benefit analysis occur within the boundaries of the laws and regulations that govern procurement. Conflicting and overlapping laws and regulations mean that government managers have some degree of discretion in their work, while raising the risk that contract managers could insert their own political values into their procurement decisions. Regulatory analysis should identify the boundaries of contract manager's discretion. Requirements definition and cost–benefit analysis can then help managers achieve public values and weigh trade-offs rather than inserting their own value preferences into the procurement process.

4.2.6 Transaction Costs and Skills

Transaction costs are the resources buyers and sellers expend to make the exchange happen, which can reduce the value that either party receives from the exchange. Our discussions in the preceding sections show that market frictions are often stronger for government purchasing. Governments often purchase in "thin" markets (Girth et al. 2012). Governments are often responsible for providing citizens with products that come with very high fixed costs relative to their marginal costs. Public values such as transparency and due process or environmental and social considerations can increase costs, because products with more quality dimensions and purchasing procedure requirements can result in higher negotiation and monitoring costs (Amirkhanyan, Kim, and Lambright 2007; Darnall, Ji, and Potoski 2017). All these frictions require transaction cost expenditures to ensure the exchange delivers value. Compared to private sector purchasing, government purchasing results in higher spending on activities to mitigate transaction costs, both for the buyer and the seller (Potoski, Petersen, and Brown 2022). Governments often buy unique products or have additional requirements for common products, which can raise transaction costs for challengers competing against incumbent sellers. The higher transaction costs frequently associated with selling to government can thus lead to markets with fewer than ideal sellers. Experience with government purchasing regulations can likewise advantage incumbent sellers against challengers.

To diagnose possible sources of transaction costs for a given purchase, contract managers need *cost estimation* skills, which is the ability to identify the prices, risks, and other costs in the production and exchange of products (Valerdi 2019). Cost estimation can include scanning the market to see if the price of a product is the same when sellers offer the same product to private clients as they do to the government. Higher prices for government buyers may lead to additional transaction costs compared to business-to-business exchanges. Cost estimation can also include process analysis to examine production inputs and processes to identify the components of production costs. There are a variety of tools and methods that aid rigorous analysis of production processes, including Six Sigma, Lean, Agile, and Total Quality Management (Sreedharan and Sunder 2018).

The skill of *process improvement* is the ability to change or eliminate activities in an exchange to improve the efficiency of the tasks and activities required to make the exchange happen. Process improvement methods offer techniques for identifying new ways of performing a task and assess whether each transaction cost expenditure required in an exchange adds value. For example, Total Quality Management relies heavily on drawing insights for process improvement from the people currently executing the process. To fully utilize the knowledge gained from cost estimation and process improvement to lower transaction costs and increased value, contract managers require the skill of *strategic thinking* – the ability to learn and apply knowledge relevant to the circumstances. In the case of contract management, the application of continuous learning involves learning about the procurement processes and how they add or subtract value in the exchange, and then applying that knowledge to deliver value. Knowing that sellers that have experience selling to the government have acquired knowledge about how to efficiently navigate exchanges with the government, contract managers can apply the skill of continuous learning to discover their insights and share that knowledge with other potential vendors to lower the transaction costs of doing business with the government.

4.3 Section Summary

In this section, we have demonstrated how our framework can be used to identify contract management skills that can address common government contracting problems and harness public value. For each of the six market frictions, we have shown how the framework can help identify examples of skills that diagnose and treat the friction itself. Our framework adds an explicit human resource perspective, which is rarely present in economic and public management scholarship on government contracting. Our framework bridges key theoretical debates on contracting, markets, and human resource management and offers actionable insights for the government contracting profession: diagnosing market frictions as the root causes of contracting problems and applying skills to address them. The added value of our framework is that rather than treating market frictions as externally imposed, buying governments can deploy human resources – the skills and knowledge of their contract management staff – to reduce and manage market frictions to harness public values.

Our framework can help analysts diagnose and treat the frictions that cause purchasing challenges. Understanding the problems and solutions can also help government scholars identify the link between circumstances, contract management activities, and skills that may harness public value from the purchase. However, there is a risk in identifying skills for market frictions separately, as we have done here for purposes of simplicity. At first glance, a wise contracting strategy might involve investing more resources, for example, in vendor training and market management to reduce the incomplete market friction. While this would potentially reduce that market competition friction, it almost certainly would also increase the transaction costs friction. Frictions, skills, and management activities are deeply interconnected. Whether it is worthwhile to deploy market management skills to train and attract suppliers depends on the benefits and costs it has for other frictions. To demonstrate the value of our framework in real-world government contracting scenarios with multiple and overlapping market frictions, in Section 5, we apply it to a common contracting challenge – quality shading.

5 The Framework Applied: Diagnosing and Treating Quality Shading

In this section, we integrate all the elements of our framework – market frictions, management activities, and skills – into a conceptual lens for analyzing contract management. We apply the framework to a common contracting challenge – quality shading, where the seller delivers a product that falls below the purchasing government's needs – to show how skilled contract managers mitigate risks that stem from market frictions. We examine quality shading because it commonly appears in discussions of contracting research (Jensen and Stonecash 2005; Hart and Moore 2008; Elkomy, Cookson, and Jones 2019). Effective contract management involves diagnosing which market friction (or combinations of frictions) gave rise to quality shading, and hence, which activities can target quality shading's root causes, and how skillful contract management can deliver a win–win outcome. We explain how different contract management approaches – formal versus relational – may emphasize the use of different contract management activities. Additionally, we examine the interdependencies between its core elements: Frictions influence the choice of investments in contract management, activities, and investments in skills, and vice versa.

We begin the section with a presentation of our framework and its three core elements in Section 5.1. In Section 5.2, we apply the framework to a concrete example to demonstrate its applicability. The framework offers value for analyses a broad range of problems. For any contract exchange, our framework can help identify why contract outcomes occurred and how management could improve outcomes under different circumstances. Fundamentally, there is no one-size-fits-all approach. Instead, contract management is a dynamic and strategic practice in which the steps to take are contingent on the larger contracting context, the actions of the seller, and the capabilities of the contract management workforce. We consider these interdependencies among the framework elements and the implications in Section 5.3. For researchers, the framework enables analyses of the interactions, including a new focus on the skills of the contract management workforce. For practitioners, such analyses can identify trade-offs among contract management activities and guide investments in the contract management workforce. Finally, Section 5.4, concludes with a summary and discussion of how the framework may guide contracting analyses.

5.1 A Framework of Frictions, Management Activities, and Skills

Our framework starts from the standard point of departure for analyzing contracting: the terms negotiated between the buyer and the seller for the quality of the product, the terms of the exchange, and the governance of exchange. Contract management is the activity that managers perform to craft the contract and execute the exchange. Ex ante management activities include defining the needs the purchase is to address, soliciting and evaluating offerings, and negotiating contract terms. Ex post management activities include exchanging resources to purchase the product, evaluating the product's performance, and engaging in the relationship over the contract duration. We also identified the range of values and costs at stake in government contracting. Product values are the qualities of the product in use, including how the product functions, and the social values that are important because of political mandates and/or sentiments of the citizenry. Process values accrue through how the exchange is executed. Likewise, government purchasing involves a range of costs – the purchase price, ownership costs, transaction costs, costs of use, and maintenance costs. The value proposition of government purchasing is complicated by the complex trade-off between all these values and costs.

We first explained the framework with a linear description connecting the activities of contract management with the values those activities aim to achieve. A drawback with this type of analysis is that the value governments derive from purchasing depends not just on what was purchased and how but also on the exchange's circumstances. Our framework uses market frictions to identify the differences in contracting challenges across different products and circumstances. A friction is a deviation from the conditions of ideal exchange – larger frictions pose larger threats to value. The sources of frictions are a lack of competition, non-fungible assets, incomplete information, incomplete property rights, externalities, and transaction costs. Government purchasing tends to occur with higher frictions than purchasing by other organizations. For example, government regulations require process and social values through purchasing, which leads to purchases with more frictions. Additional social values, for example, translate into additional product dimensions, which in turn make it harder to acquire information, define contract terms and property rights, and find capable suppliers. The upshot of additional values at stake in government purchasing results in higher costs, even when governments and businesses purchase the same products (Potoski, Petersen, and Brown 2023).

With frictions identified, the next element in our framework is management activity. Frictions are not merely exogenous constraints. They are also opportunities for choices and actions by the purchasing government and sellers. Market frictions, in other words, shape the challenges contract management aims to address. Rather than assuming that a particular seller is prone to consummate or perfunctory behavior, our framework projects that sellers may be more or less likely to behave consummately or perfunctorily under different circumstances and contract management activities. The formal contract management approach looks to mitigate the sources of frictions by writing and enforcing a more detailed contract. While this approach may clarify how the buyer and seller will produce a win–win value, specifying and enforcing contract details raises transaction costs. Moreover, no contract can fully specify the buyer and seller obligations under all contingencies, leaving them room for discretion in which each side can choose actions that benefit themselves while imposing greater costs on the other. The relational contract management approach replaces contract detail with a relationship in which the buyer and seller have incentives to cooperate and choose actions that carry costs for themselves and greater gains for their partner. The risk is that absent a detailed contract to govern the exchange, the buyer has few levers built into the contract to sanction the seller's perfunctory behavior should the virtuous cycle of cooperation not materialize.

The third element in our framework is skills, the categories of human capabilities that affect the quality of contract management activities. The skills of contract management are the ability to diagnose and treat market frictions as the root causes of contracting challenges and to perform activities that mitigate the resulting risk of lost value. Contract management executed with more skill is more likely to diagnose and treat the frictions that characterize the circumstances of the exchange and more effectively enhance value.

Our framework directs analytic attention to the sources of contract challenges. In many circumstances, frictions can be hard to discern. One of the challenges of identifying the source of a pernicious symptom is that different frictions can be the cause, and in many cases multiple frictions are present at once. Products with more quality features, for example, tend to have more information problems, and products with more information problems are also likely to require more transaction cost expenditures, like detailed contracts specifying product features along those dimensions. Using our framework for contract management can thus be a contract management skill in and of itself; a better understanding and application of our framework can help contract managers more effectively diagnose different frictions and their risks and assess and deploy contract management responses.

Our framework also calls attention to the skills in the government workforce executing the contract. Not all governments can reasonably expect their entire contract workforce to have the same diagnostic and treatment skills for all frictions. More likely, contract management personnel have specialized skills, and the contract management workforce for different governments are likely to have differently distributed diagnostic and treatment skills as well as skills for formal and relational contract management. Some governments may build expertise in the skills that accompany a more formal approach to contracting, while others may invest in skills that facilitate a relational approach. Our framework is flexible and context contingent: Governments should adapt their contract management activities to the frictions present, the resulting impact on buyer and seller behavior, and the government workforce's own skills.

5.2 Applying the Framework: Quality Shading

In this section, we apply our framework to a common contracting challenge – quality shading – to illustrate how different market frictions can give rise to a contracting challenge and how government personnel can align contract management activities and skills in response. Quality shading occurs when a seller exploits contract discretion to deliver less value than the government anticipated (Hart and Moore 2008; Elkomy, Cookson, and Jones 2019).

Throughout this Element, we have used examples of different types of products to reflect the diversity of products that governments purchase. Here, we use a frequently purchased product – information technology systems – to demonstrate the applicability of our framework.

5.2.1 Quality Shading and the Contracts' Product, Process, and Social Values

A marker of a successful contract is whether the government receives the value it anticipated when it agreed to the purchase. *Quality shading* occurs when an opportunistic seller exploits contract discretion to provide lower service quality than expected by the government (Hart, Shleifer, and Vishny 1997). Sellers have an incentive to engage in quality shading because they increase their gains by lowering production costs while receiving the same price. Sometimes these losses are easy to detect because the product fails to meet a specific performance requirement. Many governments purchase citizen relationship management (CRM) systems, an informational technology commonly referred to as customer relationship management systems in the private sector. These systems help governments keep track of and manage service interactions with citizens. Citizen relationship management purchases typically involve a combination of hardware, software, and follow-on services. Citizen relationship management can fail in a variety of ways: citizens may have a poor-quality experience interfacing with the technology, the system may intermittently not track citizens across multiple interactions, or the system might connect a citizen to a different service than the one they requested. A quality shading seller might choose not to disclose these flaws when pitching the system. Quality shading may also occur for process and social values, often in ways that are more difficult to detect. A vendor selling a CRM may have not met a set-aside requirement for the use of disadvantaged subcontractors. If the difference between what was delivered and what was promised is legally enforceable, the government may have remedy through court adjudication. Often, though, a government must accept less value because contract ambiguities prevent legal recourse or the costs of legal action are prohibitive. The CRM might not merge data systems effectively, while still requiring higher operating costs relative to the available alternatives. The seller might not have met the set-aside goal but might have come close enough that any remedy would be too risky for the government to pursue.

Quality shading can be pernicious not only in the obvious cases where the information technology system fails to function but also when the product comes close to meeting several performance, process, or social requirements. Each deviation on its own may represent a small loss for the government, yet market frictions may make fixes prohibitively costly to pursue. These losses can add up, leaving the government with substantial losses it cannot recoup.

5.2.2 Quality Shading and Conventional Contract Management

If a government fears the possibility of quality shading, a contract manager might choose to adhere advice from the conventional contracting cannon by following series of steps across the life cycle of the contract, from ex ante activities like market search and contract writing to ex post activities like evaluating product quality. Viewed as a series of steps, each activity has merit. Ex ante, inviting multiple bids through a request for proposals provides contract managers with information about options and costs. Crafting a contract with clearly specified requirements helps ensure that the seller is meeting the government's expectations, backed by a more credible threat of legal action. The more detailed contract also facilitates ex post contract management by providing a clear benchmark for determining if the product fits what the government requests. Finally, a more detailed contract facilitates resolution if quality falls below agreed upon requirements. An advantage of this standard process is its sequential comprehensiveness. At each phase of the contracting life cycle, proscribed steps are taken to mitigate risk, and if the quality shading is discovered, there is the potential hammer of legal action.

The downside of this approach is that it fails to account for the exchange context, including the product's attributes, market characteristics, and how these forces potentially influence seller behavior. For example, a government purchasing a complex CRM system may struggle to identify its precise needs (e.g., ensuring that citizens who speak different languages can effectively access the system) and describe them in a contract. The conventional contracting steps, such as specifying product details, can be time intensive and expensive. Legal action can also be costly. There is also the risk that these activities don't match the context and do little to reduce the risk of quality shading or deliver recompense. For example, a court may fail to uphold a quality shading claim if the government struggled to specify the product's requirements with sufficient precision at the outset. Fundamentally, defaulting to a rigid contract management process is a response to quality shading's symptoms and not its root causes.

5.2.3 Diagnosing Quality Shading's Market Frictions

Analyzing market frictions can help contract managers identify when quality deficiency problems are more likely to occur, allowing managers to implement appropriate treatments. Our framework starts with the use of diagnostic skills to determine the presence of frictions and contracting challenges. In the case of quality shading, three market frictions are potential drivers: incomplete information, incomplete markets, and asset-specific products. All three frictions create opportunity for perfunctory behavior to lower quality below the purchasing government's expectations.

Purchasing IT systems like a CRM can be fraught with incomplete information. The government may struggle to specify its needs in precise and specific terms, and sellers may not know how to create systems that fit the government's unique mission of providing services to all citizens instead of only those willing and able to pay. Governments often lack information ex ante (the government may not know which CRM system, or what options within a CRM system, are best for its needs) and ex post (the government may not easily know how well a CRM system serves thousands of citizens if it did not include mechanisms for surveying users' experiences). When the government lacks information, it often makes purchases where sellers have an information advantage. Sellers know more about the components and processes included in the product, they know the performance of the product, and how much time they will invest in fixing any flaws and deficiencies. Under asymmetric information, the risk of lost value is higher because the seller has an incentive to exaggerate the product's qualities, looking to dupe the buyer into overpaying up front or paying more later when the product needs to be fixed.

A second friction – incomplete markets – can likewise lead to quality shading problems. Monopolistic sellers have incentives to reveal less information about the quality features of their products and to charge higher prices for the products they sell. Without alternative sellers, the purchasing government must often accept what is offered. Some features of a CRM system may tend toward monopoly markets. For example, a CRM system might require citizens to download a specific application to access the system and then store the information on the application. More generally, IT operating system software can have high fixed costs for development but lower marginal costs for producing the software for one additional computer.

A third friction – asset-specific investments – can create quality shading problems by allowing sellers to leverage the holdup problem. Some CRM systems, as noted Section 5.2.2, are customized for processes and data that are unique to the purchasing government; whichever seller wins the contract makes the asset-specific investment to build the unique system. The government often makes its own asset-specific investments, such as by training its employees on the CRM's unique software features. Once the government makes the purchase, switching to an alternative seller means the government's investments lose value. The seller may exploit the buyer's investment for their own advantage by lowering product quality while maintaining prices. Or after the purchase has started, the seller may slow the pace of product upgrades and reduce technical support.

Each of these frictions can independently create conditions for quality shading. Combinations of frictions can also occur, sometimes with several at work in tandem. The presence of one friction can cause or exacerbate other frictions. Incomplete information can lead to incomplete contracts and costly fixes when product quality falls short. Production that requires specialized investments often leads to thin markets as fewer sellers are willing to make non-fungible production investments without assurance of making the sale. A monopolistic seller may offer products requiring buyers to make asset-specific investments to ensure their competitive advantage endures.

Exchange conditions can also vary across purchases. Purchases of the same product may occur under different frictions. Quality shading is less likely when the government looks to buy a simple product with low frictions that many sellers offer and can easily be replaced (e.g., a computer monitor). A seller can engage in quality shading only when market frictions allow, such as when contract loopholes allow the seller discretion to raise prices. Strategically deploying contract management to fit exchange conditions starts with diagnosing the presence, severity, and interdependence of frictions. Putting diagnostic skills into practice carries some costs, suggesting the need for analysis to determine their value in different contexts. Diagnosing frictions is particularly useful before the contracting process has begun. Diagnosing leads to more accurate and detailed portraits of the challenges in the future contract. If the purchasing government struggles to describe in detail the product and its attributes, odds are good that prospective sellers will have an information advantage and there may be further challenges in delineating property rights and contract terms. Diagnosing whether asset-specific investments are required is also informative – specialized investments mean that markets that initially appear competitive can quickly thin after the purchase. Diagnostic analysis that goes beyond simply counting sellers to also assessing seller capabilities sheds light on the opportunities for quality shading.

Diagnostic skills are also useful in later stages of the contract. Diagnostic skills can help governments anticipate how vendors may behave under different scenarios. Business analysis skills can identify whether sellers have business strategies that pursue longer-term gains through consummate behavior and cooperation with buyers. A company selling CRM systems, for example, may consistently look for ways to perform beyond customer expectations, perhaps by finding innovative ways to customize software (e.g., including a feature that allows citizens who speak different languages to utilize the system). Such consummate behavior, while costly to the seller in the short run, may be part of a strategy that looks to grow the business through a strong customer service reputation. To manage the contract relationship, contract analysis and business analysis can inform governments on how best to incentivize seller performance through contract terms. In addition, regulatory analysis and stakeholder mapping can help contract managers identify externalities. Cost estimation and process improvement can be utilized to determine the source of higher prices, such as whether they stem from higher transaction costs or seller performance.

The effective use of diagnostic skills identifies the underlying market frictions that create opportunities for quality shading. The next step is to design and deploy treatment skills to target quality shading's root causes.

5.2.4 Treating Quality Shading's Market Frictions: Management Approaches, Activities, and Skills

Some contract management advice suggests executing a set of management steps and activities that can be ill-suited for every circumstance (e.g., Weele 2018). As we show in this Element, however, the efficacy of a management activity depends on the exchange's underlying frictions and how it is fit with the exchange's circumstances. Skillful contract management aims to structure the exchange so that sellers have incentive to deliver value to the purchasing government, thus achieving the exchange's value potential. Positive outcomes are higher when contract management reduces market frictions, such as by improving information, increasing competition, or reducing holdups due to specialized investments in response to the frictions that create opportunities for quality shading. Enabling treatment skills occurs in two phases: first, the selection of a contract management approach (formal versus relational) and, second, the deployment of activities aligned to the approach and mapped to the specific frictions.

The value from different contract management activities and approaches depends on the context – the presence or absence of frictions. However, contracting governments may be inclined to favor management activities that fit the skills of their workforce, and previous contract management activities may enhance relevant skills. Should a government pursue a formal approach to target information asymmetries, for example, its contract management may focus on requirements definition followed by capabilities assessment. While the up-front costs of requirements definition may be high, the investment will likely provide dividends in the form of more bidders and easier assessment of alternative offers. This will also make contract design easier, notably the specification of product rules. If a contracting government utilizing a formal approach skimps on requirements definition, the opportunities for quality shading increase due to information asymmetries. Alternatively, should a government pursue a relational approach, the importance of communication skills increases. Absent a clear understanding of the product's requirements and the seller's steps to make and deliver the product, the contracting government needs to focus on ensuring that it communicates clearly what consummate and perfunctory behaviors look like. This mutual understanding of cooperative behavior enhances prospects for trust, as repeated positive interactions help solidify the relationship (Frydlinger, Hart, and Vitasek 2019).

If the contracting context is characterized by monopoly, a formal approach to contracting generally looks like regulation where allowable behaviors are proscribed in the contract to prohibit or disincentivize perfunctory behavior like quality shading. This puts a premium on contract design skills. Alternatively, if the government adopts a relational approach, the contract manager may still deploy contract design skills. However, rather than specify what behaviors are allowable, the contract might instead specify where decisions take place, based on what principles, and who has the authority to make them (e.g., the contract's governance rules). The treatment of quality shading's market frictions is similar when specialized investments are required to produce the product, although in the near term there may be multiple bidders for the contract in the first round. This apparent market competition can comfort the purchasing government that they could always return to the market should they discover quality shading. This is why diagnosis is so critical – once the contract is awarded, the chosen seller, the government, or both make asset-specific investments. Here again, the relationship may take a regulatory stance under a formal contracting approach to prevent quality shading, and a structured approach to partnership through contract design under a relational approach. Note that in the cases of incomplete markets and imperfectly fungible assets, the skill of contract design is important under both a formal and relational approach, but the focus moves from product and exchange rules under the formal approach to governance rules under the relational approach.

Whether a formal or relational approach is pursued, mitigating the risk of quality shading in the face of market frictions is not the result of ticking the boxes across the contract's life cycle. Instead, successful contract management involves accurately diagnosing the underlying frictions and designing and deploying a treatment made up of an integrated contracting approach and contract management activities to target the root causes.

5.3 Interdependencies, Contract Outcomes, and Contract Management Workforce Investments

Our application of the framework to the case of quality shading has so far held constant the potentially interdependent relationships among frictions, contract management activities, and skills. Of course, each of these constructs influences each other. Frictions influence governments' choices about whether to buy a product, which contracting approach and activities it chooses to perform, as well as how to develop and advance contract management skills in their workforce. Contract managers who regularly face thin markets may elect to emphasize the development of market management skills in their workforce. Similarly, choices governments make to invest in their contract management workforce shape the market context as contract managers interact with sellers entering and exiting the market over time. Contract managers who pursue formal approaches and regularly deploy the skill of crafting detailed and precise contracts, for example, can raise the transaction costs of the exchange. Analyses of contract management thus need to account for the many interdependencies between frictions, activities, and skills.

While there are always instances where a government purchases a novel product for the first time, often a government returns again and again to the market for similar products (e.g., the information technology systems and services we highlighted in this section). This repeated interaction is an important context for interdependencies among the core elements in our framework. To start, governments that are regular purchasers make choices about how to prepare their contract management workforce. Some of this is exogenous to the context. Standard contracting practice recommends that contract personnel have a basic set of skills, such as contract design, analytical skills, and basic knowledge of the purchasing process (Giunipero and Pearcy 2000; Karttunen 2018; Bals et al. 2019; Schulze, Bals, and Johnsen 2019). Repeated exchanges, though, may develop skills when activities are recurrent. A buying government experiencing repeated frictions may respond by investing in skills to counter the friction, its symptoms, or both. The result may be that the government is better prepared to both diagnose and respond to the friction in future purchases.

An investment in a specific skill can also influence the presence and scope of frictions. Governments that rely on a formal approach and train their workforces to develop the accompanying skills may inadvertently give rise to transaction costs, perhaps with managers investing more effort into writing and enforcing excessively detailed contracts. Similarly, sellers may have to make asset-specific investments to offer a product that meets the unique requirements mandated by a single government. Alternatively, governments that pursue a more relational approach to contracting may exacerbate information asymmetries, perhaps assuming the relationship will obviate the need for writing product and exchange rules that require the seller to share important information on the product quality and performance. Knowing that a purchasing government does not require high levels of information from bidders, an unscrupulous seller may not reveal defects about their products or promise to deliver higher product, social, or process value than they intend to. In many cases, a buying government needs a workforce with skills related to both formal and relational contracting.

5.4 Section Summary

Our framework presents the key factors for identifying why contracting outcomes occurred and what might have occurred under different circumstances – the market frictions, contract management activities, and skills that influence the range of purchasing costs and values. Each of these factors can directly influence contract outcomes. Frictions are the cause of contracting challenges. Management activities aim to reduce the frictions' causes and consequences. Skills influence the effectiveness of management activities in addressing frictions. The values from a contract are rarely the result of a single factor, and quite often the factors interact in complex ways, including how the contracting government has responded to frictions in the past. To illustrate how the framework can guide contracting analyses, we applied it to a common contracting challenge – quality shading. In doing so, we illustrate how different market frictions can give rise to contracting challenges and how government personnel can, in response, align contract management approaches, activities, and skills.

6 Conclusion

Given the magnitude and strategic importance of government purchasing, contracting is perhaps the most fertile ground for improving government performance. When managed effectively, government contracting can acquire products more quickly, cheaply, and of higher quality than if made by governments themselves, all while advancing public values like transparency, equity, and accountability. But government contracting is fraught with challenges stemming from the market frictions that threaten to undermine this potential for improved public value. The purchasing government may be uncertain about which products to buy, or there may be only one seller offering a product (Girth et al. 2012). Sometimes governments adopt policies and practices, often with good intentions, that exacerbate risks rather than mitigate them, such as when the government requires vendor qualifications that are so stringent that competition evaporates. Effective contract management can diagnose and treat market frictions and thereby reduce the risk of lost value. Contract management is a strategic exercise – an integrated set of choices about which approach and activities to undertake in the presence of market frictions, actions of the sellers, and skills within the government's workforce.

We first present implications that are relevant for scholarly and practical analyses and then offer some additional implications specific to each. Effective scholarly and practical analyses need to make a precise diagnosis of the underlying frictions that cause common contracting challenges and identify potential management solutions. The skills of contract management include diagnosing the presence and extent of market frictions, determining how frictions influence seller behavior, and treating the frictions with management activities. Understanding the problem and potential solutions can also help contract analysts identify the human skills that fit the circumstances. Without this knowledge, contract scholars and managers are, at best, treating symptoms rather than addressing their causes. Frictions can have three types of negative consequences. First, market frictions may prevent exchanges from occurring even when both the buyer and the seller would have been better off had the exchange happened. Second, frictions may require the buyer and seller to spend additional resources to make the exchange happen, thereby reducing the gains realized from the exchange. Finally, market frictions increase the risk that an exchange will fail. Failure means that the buyer, seller, or both experience losses greater than the value received from the exchange.

For scholars and practitioners, our framework facilitates analyses of cause-and-effect and conditional relationships among market frictions, contract management activities, and skills. The effect of one factor may depend on the levels of other factors. For example, improving relational skills might be more valuable in high-friction conditions with long-term partnership contracts while yielding lower returns in low-friction settings, such as spot market transactions for commodities. The effectiveness of management activities varies significantly with skill levels – what may be ineffective with low skills could yield substantial benefits when performed with higher skills. The framework enables analyses of these complex relationships, offering deeper insights into the payoffs and trade-offs among contracting strategies.

6.1 Implications for Research

For contracting research, our framework introduces both market frictions and skills as important components of government contract outcomes. Research on government contracting requires a comprehensive approach that covers frictions, management activities, and skills, and facilitates assessing their interdependencies in impacting contract outcomes. In addition, our framework allows contracting scholars to place government contracting in the broader social science context, facilitating exchange of conceptual insights with areas such as governance, transaction costs and the boundaries of the firm, contract theory, and institutional design and performance.

Our framework also suggests that future research should account for the human resource dimension of contracting. Much of the research on contracting focuses on product attributes, market conditions, and contract design, often overlooking the people who undertake the tasks of managing the contract. A lesson from the implementation literature is that the professionalization of the workforce charged with implementing public programs has a demonstrable impact on outcomes (Kroll and Moynihan 2015). Our framework builds from that insight by incorporating human resources more explicitly into government contract management. The effectiveness of contract management depends in part on the skills of the managers who decide which activities to pursue, and the skill with which they are implemented. Another insight from our framework is that simply measuring skills is insufficient because the impact of skills depends on the other factors. A skilled contracting workforce is one that effectively diagnoses and treats market frictions by writing contracts and developing relationships that effectively address the contracting challenge and maximizes public value from the purchase.

Our framework also indicates that contract analyses need to address the public values governments pursue and the context of the exchange. Every government purchase puts multiple values at stake: product value in how well the product performs, process value in how the purchase is executed, and broader social value. Focusing narrowly on one value dimension risks overlooking the trade-offs across the types of values. Different combinations of management activities and skills are likely to deliver different types of value in different contexts. A full assessment of values also necessitates a more explicit focus on how the buyer and seller can influence the value and costs each receives from the purchase. The buyer's management activities may increase value to the government while incurring higher costs on the seller, and vice versa. When purchasing under circumstances of incomplete information, the government buyer may choose to address this market friction using a formal approach. Writing a more complete contract that specifies the seller's obligations to collect and share data and participate in weekly status meetings increases the seller's transaction costs. To account for the added costs, the seller may offer higher prices, in turn, reducing the buyer's value. Rather than investigate whether formal or relational contracts are superior in all contexts, future research should examine the value trade-offs for both parties that arise under different market frictions, management activities, and contracting contexts.

Government contracting research faces challenges common to many areas of social science: samples are often small and nonrepresentative, cause and effect are difficult to disentangle, key theoretical concepts defy systematic empirical measurement, to name only a few. This Element identifies additional challenges to scholarly inquiry on government contracting. Market frictions often necessitate more extensive contract management activities, such as market-building initiatives or supplier training. At the same time, performing these activities can increase skills among the managers performing them, such as when managers gain expertise in contract writing or monitoring as they perform these tasks. Likewise, managers' skills can influence the deployment and efficacy of activities, with governments gravitating toward actions that harness their capabilities. There are no simple solutions to these challenges, of course.

Future research should examine the multiple causal interdependencies among frictions, skills, and management activities to provide a more complete account of government contracting. Examining any one of these factors in isolation risks offering, at best, an incomplete picture – and, at worst, a misleading account of the mechanisms shaping contract outcomes. Our framework calls for research designs that explicitly model the causal relationships and interaction effects among skills, frictions, and management activities, rather than assuming each operate in isolation. Our Element offers a theoretical framework that can facilitate the integration of insights from various analytic methods, including single and comparative case studies, laboratory and field experiments, surveys, and large sample empirical research, with each study's strengths and weaknesses balancing the strength and weaknesses of others. Different research methods and approaches can contribute to accumulating knowledge about frictions, skills, and management activities. By systematically addressing the core components in our framework – frictions, skills, and management activities – future research can advance the understanding of causal relationships in shaping contract performance and shed light on how contracting success depends on aligning skills and management activities with the frictions characterizing each exchange.

6.2 Implications for Practice

Our framework looks to guide the practice of contract management by helping managers identify contract challenges and deploy management activities to fit the circumstances. Perhaps the most fundamental contract management activity is understanding the contracting challenge that arises from the circumstances of a particular purchase. Getting the right diagnosis of contracting challenges is essential for effectively addressing them. This task is complex because many government purchases are characterized by multiple frictions that appear in many different combinations that can also depend on their own contract management activities and skills of the contracting workforce. Our framework offers contract managers a way to diagnose and treat contracting problems with greater nuance and precision. The approach starts by assessing the presence and severity of market frictions as the root causes of contracting challenges and then identifying management activities in response to the underlying contract problem. Deploying management activities to address frictions is complicated by the fact that different management activities, as we have seen, can address the same contracting challenge, sometimes even with the same cost–benefit ratio.

Common prescriptions for contracting practice identify activities managers should perform for all purchases regardless of the circumstances. Professional contract management training programs for civil servants focus on topics such as regulatory and legal compliance and contract management activities drawn from business school purchasing curricula (Van Weele 2018). Such guidance, as we have discussed, is unlikely to deliver the best value. Our framework offers guidance for improving contract management: The efficacy of any contracting activity depends on the presence of frictions and the skills of the contracting government's workforce. Governments may choose management activities that reflect existing skills; a workforce with more communication and business analysis skills is more likely to pursue relational contracting approaches, particularly when purchasing products with difficult-to-measure qualities and asset-specific investments. But a government may also cultivate certain skills based on the types of purchases it frequently makes. For instance, when frequently purchasing products using a relational contracting approach, a government may benefit from building communication skills. Meanwhile, governments resorting to a more formal contract approach could improve contract design skills focused on writing detailed product rules. Our framework helps governments pursue skills to suit the context of their purchases and the management activities that improve value for the purchase.

Our framework also highlights how contract managers can weigh different types of public value in government purchases. These values relate not only to the function of the product but also to the process through which it is purchased and broader social values the purchase may provide. Government contract managers often face difficult choices, as public procurement rules can amplify market frictions and trade-offs among competing public values. For example, a requirement to conduct a transparent procurement process with open access and equal treatment for all vendors may promote process values while resulting in lower product value, as governments may end up with products or suppliers they did not initially prefer. This Element offers a systematic account of different types of public values at stake in government contracting. Contract managers can use our framework in applied settings to assess which values are central to their specific purchase and the trade-offs among them. Over time, this can lead to a shared language for the different types of value at stake with government contracting.

Finally, contract management is not merely a technical or administrative task – it is also a strategic exercise, as emphasized at the outset of this section. Our framework shows that effective contract management involves a series of informed choices: how to effectively diagnose market frictions, which management activities to apply in response, what skills to apply or develop, and which public values to prioritize in each purchase. This Element highlights that there is no single set of practices that apply to every purchase. Rather, a core insight for practitioners is that effective contract management requires situational analyses – an ability to diagnose the context of the exchange, understand the frictions involved, recognize the available skills, and make decisions accordingly. By viewing contract management through this lens, managers can approach purchasing as a strategic effort to align management activities with the frictions, skills, and public values central to each purchase.

References

Akerlof, G. A. (1970). The market for "lemons": Quality uncertainty and the market mechanism. *The Quarterly Journal of Economics*, 84(3), 488–500.

Akerlof, G. A. 1974. The Market for 'Lemons': Quality Uncertainty and the Market Mechanism. *Quarterly Journal of Economics*. 84 (3), 488–500.

Alchian, A. A., & Demsetz, H. (1973). The property right paradigm. *The Journal of Economic History*, 33(1), 16–27.

Amirkhanyan, A. A. (2011). What is the effect of performance measurement on perceived accountability effectiveness in state and local government contracts? *Public Performance and Management Review*, 35, 303–339.

Amirkhanyan, A. A., Cheon, O., Davis, J. A., Meier, K. J., & Wang, F. (2019). Citizen participation and its impact on performance in US nursing homes. *The American Review of Public Administration*, 49(7), 840–854.

Amirkhanyan, A. A., Kim, H. J., & Lambright, K. T. (2007). Putting the pieces together: A comprehensive framework for understanding the decision to contract out and contractor performance. *International Journal of Public Administration*, 30(6–7), 699–725.

Amirkhanyan, A. A., Kim, H. J., & Lambright, K. T. (2010). Do relationships matter? Assessing the association between relationship design and contractor performance. *Public Performance and Management Review*, 34(2), 189–220.

Amirkhanyan, A. A., Kim, H. J., & Lambright, K. T. (2012). Closer than "arms length": Understanding the factors associated with collaborative contracting. *The American Review of Public Administration*, 42(3), 341–66.

Andersen, L. B., Jørgensen, T. B., Kjeldsen, A. M., Pedersen, L. H., & Vrangbæk, K. (2012). Public value dimensions: Developing and testing a multi-dimensional classification. *International Journal of Public Administration*, 35(11), 715–728.

Andersson, F. & Jordahl, H. (2011). Outsourcing public services: Ownership, competition, quality and contracting. Working Paper No. 874, Research Institute of Industrial Economics (IFN).

Anguelov, L. G. (2020). Monitoring arrangements for outsourced public services: The importance of service characteristics for the distribution of oversight responsibilities. *International Public Management Journal*, 23(2), 252–275.

Arrow, K. J., & Hahn, F. H. (1971). General Competitive Analysis. San Francisco: Holden-Day.

Axelrod, R., & Hamilton, W. D. (1981). The evolution of cooperation. *Science*, 211(4489), 1390–1396.

References

Baker, G., Gibbons, R., & Murphy, K. J. (2002). Relational contracts and the theory of the firm. *The Quarterly Journal of Economics*, 117(1), 39–84.

Bals, L., Schulze, H., Kelly, S., & Stek, K. (2019). Purchasing and supply management (PSM) competencies: Current and future requirements. *Journal of Purchasing and Supply Management*, 25(5), 100572.

Barney, J. (1991). Firm resources and sustained competitive advantage. *Journal of Management*, 17(1), 99–120.

Bel, G., & Fageda, X. (2009). Factors explaining local privatization: A meta-regression analysis. *Public Choice*, 139, 105–119.

Bel, G., Fageda, X., & Warner, M. E. (2010). Is private production of public services cheaper than public production? A meta-regression analysis of solid waste and water services. *Journal of Policy Analysis and Management*, 29(3), 553–577.

Bennmarker, H., Grönqvist, E. and Öckert, B. (2013). Effects of contracting out employment services: Evidence from a randomized experiment. *Journal of Public Economics*, vol. 98: 68–84.

Bozeman, B. (2002). Public-value failure: When efficient markets may not do. *Public Administration Review*, 62(2), 145–161.

Brogaard, L., Petersen, O. H., & Madsen, M. S. (2025). Skills and knowledge for public contract management: A taxonomy and integrative framework. *Perspectives on Public Management and Governance*, 8, 172–186.

Brown, T., Kim, Y. W., & Roberts, A. (2015). Product characteristics, market conditions and contract type: US department of defense use of fixed-price and cost reimbursement contracts. *Acquisition Research Program*. https://dair.nps.edu/handle/123456789/2641.

Brown, T. L., & Matthew Potoski (2003). Transaction costs and institutional explanations for government service production decisions. *Journal of Public Administration Research and Theory* 13 (4), 441–468.

Brown, T., & Potoski, M. (2006). Contracting for management: Assessing management capacity under alternative service delivery arrangements. *Journal on Public Analysis and Management*, 25, 323–346.

Brown, T. L., Potoski, M., & Slyke, D. V. (2016). Managing complex contracts: A theoretical approach. *Journal of Public Administration Research and Theory*, 26(2), 294–308.

Brown, T. L., Matthew P., & David M. V. S. (2018). Complex contracting: Management challenges and solutions. Public Administration Review 78 (5), 739–747.

Brunjes, B. M. (2022). Your competitive side is calling: An analysis of Florida contract performance. *Public Administration Review*, 82(1), 83–101.

Brunjes, B. M., & Rodriguez-Plesa, E. (2024). Equity in government contracting: Analyzing the performance of small disadvantaged businesses. *Public Administration Review*, 84(3), 484–499.

Bryson, J. M., Crosby, B. C., & Bloomberg, L. (2014). Public value governance: Moving beyond traditional public administration and the new public management. *Public Administration Review*, 74(4), 445–456.

Carnochan, S., McBeath, B., Chuang, E., & Austin, M. J., (2019). Perspectives of public and nonprofit managers on communications in human services contracting. *Public Performance and Management Review*, 42, 657–684.

Casady, C. B., Petersen, O. H., & Brogaard, L. (2023). Public procurement failure: The role of transaction costs and government capacity in procurement cancellations. *Public Management Review*, 1–28.

Cheetham, G., & Chivers, G. (1996). Towards a holistic model of professional competence. *Journal of European Industrial Training*, 20(5), 20–30.

Chen, Y.-C., & Perry, J. (2003). Outsourcing for e-government: Managing for success. *Public Performance and Management Review*, 26, 404–421.

Cooper, P. J. (2002). Governing by Contract: Challenges and Opportunities for Public Managers. New York: Sage.

Danish National Audit (2020). Rigsrevisionens beretning afgivet til Folketinget med Statsrevisorernes bemærkninger Ændringer i sygehusbyggerierne – 11/2019. www.rigsrevisionen.dk/Media/637830381019749820/SR1119.pdf.

Darnall, N., Ji, H., & Potoski, M. (2017). Institutional design of ecolabels: Sponsorship signals rule strength. *Regulation & Governance*, 11(4), 438–450.

Datta-Chaudhuri, M. (1990). Market failure and government failure. *Journal of Economic Perspectives*, 4(3), 25–39.

David, R. J., & Han, S. K. (2004). A systematic assessment of the empirical support for transaction cost economics. *Strategic Management Journal*, 25(1), 39–58.

De Schepper, S., Elvira H. & Michaël D. (2015). Understanding pre-contractual transaction costs for Public–Private Partnership infrastructure projects. *International Journal of Project Management* 33 (4), 932–946.

Deist, F. D. L., & Winterton, J. (2005). What is competence? *Human Resource Development International*, 8(1), 27–46.

Derwik, P., & Hellström, D. (2017). Competence in supply chain management: A systematic review. *Supply Chain Management: An International Journal*, 22(2), 200–218.

Dimand, A. M., Abutabenjeh, S., Rodriguez-Plesa, E., Alkadry, M. G., & Bruns Ali, S. (2023a). Human capital drivers of employee intent to innovate: The case of public procurement professionals. *Review of Public Personnel Administration*, 43(4), 727–753.

Dimand, A. M., & Neshkova, M. I. (2024). Buying green in US local government: Internal commitment and responsiveness to external pressures. *Public Administration*, 102(2), 644–667.

Dimand, A. M., Patrucco, A. S., Rodriguez-Plesa, E., & Hiriscau, A. M. (2023b). Social equity in federal contracting during emergencies: A portfolio management perspective. *Public Administration Review*, 83(5), 1319–1338.

Domberger, S., & Jensen, P. (1997). Contracting out by the public sector: Theory, evidence, prospects. *Oxford Review of Economic Policy*, 13(4), 67–78.

Domingos, F. D., Heinrich, C. J., Saussier, S., & Shiva, M. (2025). The interplay of discretion and complexity in public contracting and renegotiations. *Journal of Public Administration Research and Theory*, 35(2), 148–163.

Dyer, J. H., & Chu, W. (2003). The role of trustworthiness in reducing transaction costs and improving performance: Empirical evidence from the United States, Japan, and Korea. *Organization Science*, 14(1), 57–68.

Egede Hansen, G., Bel, G., & Helby Petersen, O. (2023). The unequal distribution of consequences of contracting out: Female, low-skilled, and young workers pay the highest price. *Journal of Public Administration Research and Theory*, 33(3), 434–452.

Elkomy, S., Cookson, G., & Jones, S. (2019). Cheap and dirty: The effect of contracting out cleaning on efficiency and effectiveness. *Public Administration Review*, 79(2), 193–202.

Fama, E. F., & Jensen, M. C. (1983). Separation of ownership and control. *The Journal of Law and Economics*, 26(2), 301–325.

Fernandez, S. (2007). What works best when contracting for services? An analysis of contracting performance at the local level in the US. *Public Administration*, 85, 1119–1141.

Frydlinger, D., Hart, O., & Vitasek, K. (2019). A new approach to contracts. *Harvard Business Review*, 97(5), 116–125.

Frydlinger, D., Vitasek, K., Bergman, J., & Cummins, T. (2021). Contracting in the New Economy: Using Relational Contracts to Boost Trust and Collaboration in Strategic Business Relationships. London: Palgrave Macmillan.

Getha-Taylor, H. (2008). Identifying collaborative competencies. *Review of Public Personnel Administration*, 28(2), 103–119.

Girth, A. M., Hefetz, A., Johnston, J. M., & Warner, M. E. (2012). Outsourcing public service delivery: Management responses in noncompetitive markets. *Public Administration Review*, 72(6), 887–900.

Giunipero, L. C., & Pearcy, D. H. (2000). World-class purchasing skills: An empirical investigation. *Journal of Supply Chain Management*, 36(3), 4–13.

Goldsmith, S. (1997). *The Twenty-First Century City: Resurrecting Urban America*. Washington, DC: Regnery.

Gubbins, C., & Dooley, L. (2021). Delineating the tacit knowledge-seeking phase of knowledge sharing: The influence of relational social capital components. *Human Resource Development Quarterly*, 32(3), 319–348.

Gutiérrez-Meave, R., Zhang, S., Carr, J. B., & Siciliano, M. D. (2025). Integrating formal and relational contracting: The link between network structure and contract design in interlocal collaboration agreements. *Public Administration* (early view).

Hart, O. (2009). Hold-up, asset ownership, and reference points. *The Quarterly Journal of Economics*, 124(1), 267–300.

Hart, O., & Moore, J. (1988). Incomplete contracts and renegotiation. *Econometrica*, 755–785.

Hart, O., & Moore, J. (2007). Incomplete contracts and ownership: Some new thoughts. *American Economic Review*, 97(2), 182–186.

Hart, O., & Moore, J. (2008). Contracts as reference points. *The Quarterly Journal of Economics*, 123(1), 1–48.

Hart, O., Shleifer, A., & Vishny, R. W. (1997). The proper scope of government: Theory and an application to prisons. *The Quarterly Journal of Economics*, 112(4), 1127–1161.

Hartmann, A., Roehrich, J., Frederiksen, L., & Davies, A. (2014). Procuring complex performance: The transition process in public infrastructure. *International Journal of Operations and Production Management*, 34, 174–194.

Holmström, B. (1979). Moral hazard and observability. *The Bell Journal of Economics*, 4, 74–91.

Jensen, P. H., & Stonecash, R. E. (2005). Incentives and the efficiency of public sector-outsourcing contracts. *Journal of Economic Surveys*, 19(5), 767–787.

Joaquin, E. M., & Greitens, T. J. (2012). Contract management capacity breakdown? An analysis of US local governments. *Public Administration Review*, 72(6), 807–816.

Johnston, J. M., & Girth, A. M. (2012). Government contracts and "managing the market": Exploring the costs of strategic management responses to weak vendor competition. *Administration and Society*, 44, 3–29.

Jørgensen, T. B., & Bozeman, B. (2002). Public values lost? Comparing cases on contracting out from Denmark and the United States. *Public Management Review*, 4(1), 63–81.

Karttunen, E., (2018). Purchasing and supply management skills revisited: An extensive literature review. *Benchmarking*, 25, 3906–3934.

Kelman, S. (1990). *Procurement and Public Management: The Fear of Discretion and the Quality of Government Performance*. Washington, DC: AEI Press.

References

Kettl, D. F. (2010). Governance, contract management and public management. In The New Public Governance? (pp. 255–270). New York: Routledge.

Kim, Y. W., & Brown, T. L. (2012). The importance of contract design. *Public Administration Review*, 72(5), 687–696.

Kroll, A., & Moynihan, D. P. (2015). Does training matter? Evidence from performance management reforms. *Public Administration Review*, 75(3), 411–420.

Lamothe, M., & Lamothe, S. (2012). What determines the formal versus relational nature of local government contracting? *Urban Affairs Review*, 48, 322–353.

Langemark, D. H., & Midtiby, J. S. (2024, November 26). Milliardforsinkelser og utætte tage: Her er syv danske sygehusbyggerier, der var knap så "super." Danish Broadcasting Corporation. www.dr.dk/nyheder/indland/milliardforsinkelser-og-utaette-tage-her-er-syv-danske-sygehusbyggerier-der-var-knap.

Levin, J., & Tadelis, S. (2010). Contracting for government services: Theory and evidence from US cities. *The Journal of Industrial Economics*, 58(3), 507–541.

Li, J., Liu, B., Wang, D., & Casady, C. B. (2024). The effects of contractual and relational governance on public-private partnership sustainability. *Public Administration*, 102(4), 1418–1449.

Lo, D., Zanarone, G., & Ghosh, M. (2022). Contracting to (dis)incentivize? An integrative transaction-cost approach on how contracts govern specific investments. *Strategic Management Journal*, 43(8), 1528–1555.

Mahoney, J. T., & Qian, L. (2013). Market frictions as building blocks of an organizational economics approach to strategic management. *Strategic Management Journal*, 34(9), 1019–1041.

Malacina, I., Karttunen, E., Jääskeläinen, A. et al. (2022). Capturing the value creation in public procurement: A practice-based view. *Journal of Purchasing and Supply Management*, 28(2), 100745.

Marvel, Mary K., and Howard P. Marvel. "Outsourcing oversight: A comparison of monitoring for in-house and contracted services." Public Administration Review 67, no. 3 (2007): 521–530.

McClelland, D. C. (1973). Testing for competence rather than for "intelligence." *American Psychologist*, 28(1), 1.

McCue, C. P., Prier, E., & Steinfeld, J. M. (2018). Establishing the foundational elements of a public procurement body of knowledge. *Journal of Strategic Contracting and Negotiation*, 4, 233–251.

McKevitt, D., Davis, P., Woldring, R. et al. (2012). An exploration of management competencies in public sector procurement. *Journal of Public Procurement*, 12, 333–355.

Michelsen, O., & de Boer, L. (2009). Green procurement in Norway; a survey of practices at the municipal and county level. *Journal of Environmental Management*, 91, 160–167.

Moore, M. H. (1994). Public value as the focus of strategy. *Australian Journal of Public Administration*, 53(3), 296–303.

OECD. (2023). Government at a Glance 2023. Paris: OECD.

Olesen, H. K., & Junker, S. (2024, February 21). Kritik af gigant-udlicitering i Forsvaret: Anede ikke, hvordan ISS brugte pengene. https://fagbladet3f.dk/anede-ikke-hvordan-iss-brugte-pengene/.

Petersen, O. H., Baekkeskov, E., Potoski, M., & Brown, T. L. (2019). Measuring and managing ex ante transaction costs in public sector contracting. *Public Administration Review*, 79(5), 641–650.

Petersen, O. H., Potoski, M., & Brown, T. L. (2022). Businesses' transaction costs when contracting with governments: The impact of product complexity and public contract management experience. *International Public Management Journal*, 25(5), 741–766.

Piatak, J., & Jensen, C. (2024). Public values and sector service delivery preferences: Public preferences on contracting from simple to complex human services. *Public Administration Review*, 84 (5), 948–965.

Poppo, L., & Zenger, T. (2002). Do formal contracts and relational governance function as substitutes or complements? *Strategic Management Journal*, 23(8), 707–725.

Potoski, M., Petersen, O. H., & Brown, T. L. (2023). Same product, different price: Experimental evidence on the transaction cost expenditures of selling to governments and firms. *Public Administration Review*, 83(3), 623–638.

Prahalad, C. K. & Gary H. (2009). The core competence of the corporation. In Knowledge and strategy, pp. 41–59. Routledge.

Robinson, J. (1934). Economics of Imperfect Competition. New York: The Macmillan.

Romzek, B. S., & Johnston, J. M. (2002). Effective contract implementation and management: A preliminary model. *Journal of Public Administration Research and Theory*, 12, 423–453.

Savas, E. S. (1987). Privatization and prisons. *Vand. L. Rev.* 40, 889–899.

Schulze, H., Bals, L., & Johnsen, T. E. (2019). Individual competences for sustainable purchasing and supply management (SPSM) A literature and practice perspective. *International Journal of Physical Distribution & Logistics Management*, 49(3), 287–304.

Shaoul, J., Stafford, A., & Stapleton, P. (2006). Highway robbery? A financial analysis of design, build, finance and operate (DBFO) in UK roads. *Transport Reviews*, 26(3), 257–274.

Smith, V. L. (1962). An experimental study of competitive market behavior. *Journal of Political Economy*, 70(2), 111–137.

Smith, A. (2000). The Wealth of Nations. New York: Modern Library Classics.

Snider, K. F., & Rendon, R. G. (2012). Public procurement: Public administration and public service perspectives. *Journal of Public Affairs Education*, 18(2), 327–348.

Sreedharan V. R., & Sunder M. V. (2018). Critical success factors of TQM, Six Sigma, Lean and Lean Six Sigma: A literature review and key findings. *Benchmarking: An International Journal*, 25(9), 3479–3504.

Stek, K., & Schiele, H. (2021). How to train supply managers – necessary and sufficient purchasing skills leading to success. *Journal of Purchasing and Supply Management*, 27(4), 100700.

Stiglitz, J. E. (2010). Government failure vs. market failure: Principles of regulation. In E. J. Balleisen & D. A. Moss (eds.), Government and Markets: Toward a New Theory of Regulation (pp. 13–51). New York: Cambridge University Press.

Stiglitz, J. E., & Rosengard, J. K. (2015). Economics of the Public Sector: Fourth International Student Edition. New York: WW Norton.

Tadelis, S. (1999). What's in a Name? Reputation as a Tradeable Asset. *American Economic Review*, 89(3), 548–563.

Tadelis, S. (2012). Public procurement design: Lessons from the private sector. *International Journal of Industrial Organization*, 30(3), 297–302.

Tassabehji, R., & Moorhouse, A. (2008). The changing role of procurement: Developing professional effectiveness. *Journal of Purchasing and Supply Management*, 14(1), 55–68.

Tirole, J. (1999). Incomplete contracts: Where do we stand? *Econometrica*, 67(4), 741–781.

Turco, A. L., & Maggioni, D. (2022). The knowledge and skill content of production complexity. *Research Policy*, 51(8), 104059.

Valerdi, R. (2019). Cost estimation toolset. In Evolving Toolbox for Complex Project Management (pp. 61–75). Florida: Auerbach.

Van Slyke, D. M. (2007). Agents or stewards: Using theory to understand the government-nonprofit social service contracting relationship. *Journal of Public Administration Research and Theory*, 17(2), 157–187.

Warren, P. L. (2014). Contracting officer workload, incomplete contracting, and contractual terms. *The RAND Journal of Economics*, 45(2), 395–421.

Weele, A. J. V. (2018). Purchasing and Supply Chain Management. Andover: Cengage Learning.

Weick, K. E (1979). The Social Psychology of Organizing. New York: McGraw-Hill.

Williams, E. W., & Coase, R. H. (1964). The regulated industries-discussion. *American Economic Review*, 54(3), 192–197.

Williamson, O. E. (1979). Transaction-cost economics: The governance of contractual relations. *The Journal of Law and Economics*, 22(2), 233–61.

Williamson, O. E. (1981). The economics of organization: The transaction cost approach. *American Journal of Sociology*, 87(3), 548–577.

Williamson, O. E. (1985). The Economic Institutions of Capitalism. New York: Free Press.

Williamson, O. E. (1996). The Mechanisms of Governance. Oxford: Oxford University Press.

Wright, P. M., Dunford, B. B., & Snell, S. A. (2001). Human resources and the resource based view of the firm. *Journal of Management*, 27(6), 701–721.

Acknowledgments

This research was supported by the Independent Research Fund Denmark [Grant no.: 9061- 00020B]

Cambridge Elements

Public and Nonprofit Administration

Robert Christensen
Brigham Young University

Robert Christensen is the George W. Romney Professor of Public and Nonprofit Management at Brigham Young University.

Jaclyn Piatak
University of North Carolina at Charlotte

Jaclyn Piatak is co-editor of NVSQ and Professor of Political Science and Public Administration at the University of North Carolina at Charlotte.

Rosemary O'Leary
University of Kansas

Rosemary O'Leary is the Edwin O. Stene Distinguished Professor Emerita of Public Administration at the University of Kansas.

About the Series

The foundation of this series are cutting-edge contributions on emerging topics and definitive reviews of keystone topics in public and nonprofit administration, especially those that lack longer treatment in textbook or other formats. Among keystone topics of interest for scholars and practitioners of public and nonprofit administration, it covers public management, public budgeting and finance, nonprofit studies, and the interstitial space between the public and nonprofit sectors, along with theoretical and methodological contributions, including quantitative, qualitative and mixed-methods pieces.

The Public Management Research Association

The Public Management Research Association improves public governance by advancing research on public organizations, strengthening links among interdisciplinary scholars, and furthering professional and academic opportunities in public management.

Cambridge Elements

Public and Nonprofit Administration

Elements in the Series

Redefining Development: Resolving Complex Challenges in a Global Context
2nd edition
Jessica Kritz

Experts in Government: The Deep State from Caligula to Trump and Beyond
Donald F. Kettl

New Public Governance as a Hybrid: A Critical Interpretation
Laura Cataldi

Can Governance be Intelligent?: An Interdisciplinary Approach and Evolutionary Modelling for Intelligent Governance in the Digital Age
Eran Vigoda-Gadot

The Courts and the President: Judicial Review of Presidentially Directed Action
Charles Wise

Standing Up for Nonprofits: Advocacy on Federal, Sector-wide Issues
Alan J. Abramson and Benjamin Soskis

Topics in Public Administration: Perspectives from Computational Social Sciences and Corpus Linguistics
Richard M. Walker, Jiasheng Zhang and Yanto Chandra

Public Service Explained: The Role of Citizens in Value Creation
Greta Nasi, Stephen Osborne, Maria Cucciniello and Tie Cui

Court-Ordered Community Service: The Experiences of Community Organizations and Community Service Workers
Rebecca Nesbit, Su Young Choi and Jody Clay-Warner

Sustainable Inclusion through Performance-Driven Practices: An Evidence-Based, Dynamic Systems Framework
Ruth Sessler Bernstein and Paul Salipante

Bureaucratic Resistance in Times of Democratic Backsliding
João V. Guedes-Neto and B. Guy Peters

Managing Public Sector Contracts: Market Frictions and Human Resources Solutions
Matthew Potoski, Ole Helby Petersen, Lena Brogaard and Trevor Brown

A full series listing is available at: www.cambridge.org/EPNP

Printed by Integrated Books International,
United States of America